THE CAST

A

Goodman Ace
Roy Acuff
Ansel Adams
Henry Brooks Adams
John Quincy Adams
Mortimer Adler
Eddie Albert
(Amos) Bronson Alcott
Sir Hardy Amies
Marian Anderson
James B. Angell
Walter Annenberg
Susan B. Anthony

Elizabeth Arden
Fred Astaire
Brooke Astor
Mary Astor
Lady Nancy Astor
Gertrude Atherton
Clement Attlee

B

Enid Bagnold
John Bardeen
Natalie Clifford Barney
Ethel Barrymore

Bernard Baruch
James Beard
Lord William
    Beaverbrook
Sir Thomas Beecham
Sir Max Beerbohm
Melvin Belli
David Ben-Gurion
Jack Benny
Bernard Berenson
Irving Berlin
Eubie Blake
Daniel Boone
Daniel Boorstin
William Booth
Victor Borge
Jorge Luis Borges
Omar Bradley
Louis D. Brandeis
William J. Brennan
Pearl Buck
Luis Buñuel

George Burns
John Burroughs
William Burroughs
Vannevar Bush

C

John Cage
Elias Canetti
Thomas Carlyle
Lillian Carter
Barbara Cartland
Pablo Casals
Marcus Porcius Cato
Marc Chagall
Coco Chanel
Charlie Chaplin
John Cheever
Maurice Chevalier
Julia Child
Agatha Christie
Sir Winston Churchill

OLDER
AND
WISER

OLDER
AND
WISER

716 Memorable Quotes from
Those Who Have Lived the Longest
and Seen the Most

SELECTED BY

Gretchen B. Dianda and
Betty J. Hofmayer

BALLANTINE BOOKS / NEW YORK

Copyright © 1995 by Gretchen B. Dianda and Betty J. Hofmayer

Foreword copyright © 1995 by Random House, Inc.

All rights reserved under International and Pan-American Copyright Conventions. Published in the United States by Ballantine Books, a division of Random House, Inc., New York, and simultaneously in Canada by Random House of Canada Limited, Toronto.

Library of Congress Catalog Card Number: 94-96603
ISBN: 0-345-38505-5

Cover design by David Stevenson
Text design by Mary A. Wirth

Manufactured in the United States of America
First Edition: May 1995
10 9 8 7 6 5 4

Paul Claudel
Georges Clemenceau
Elizabeth Coatsworth
Colette
Alistair Cooke
Lady Diana Cooper
Aaron Copland
Le Corbusier
Katharine Cornell
Norman Corwin
Jacques Cousteau
Malcolm Cowley
Hume Cronyn
Imogen Cunningham

Charles A. Dawes
Dorothy Day
Charles de Gaulle
Agnes de Mille
Helene Deutsch
John Dewey
Marlene Dietrich
Dorothy Dix
William O. Douglas
W. E. B. Dubois
Marcel Duchamp
Will Durant
Marguerite Duras

D

Salvador Dali
Clarence Darrow
Robertson Davies
Bette Davis

E

Richard Eberhart
Thomas Alva Edison
Charles William Eliot
Queen Mother
  Elizabeth

Havelock Ellis
Sam Ervin
Dame Edith Evans

Robert Frost
J. William Fulbright
Buckminster Fuller

F

Clifton Fadiman
Millicent Fenwick
James E. Fitzsimmons
Abraham Flexner
Le Bovier de Fontenelle
Gerald R. Ford
Henry Ford
E. M. Forster
Harry E. Fosdick
Anatole France
Polly Francis
Felix Frankfurter
Benjamin Franklin
Sigmund Freud
Milton Friedman
Erich Fromm

G

John Kenneth
   Galbraith
Greta Garbo
John Nance Garner
Jean Paul Getty
André Gide
Sir John Gielgud
Hermione Gingold
William Gladstone
Johann von Goethe
William Golding
Samuel Goldwyn
Ruth Gordon
Maurice Goudeket
Martha Graham
Cary Grant

Robert Graves
Theodore F. Green
Graham Greene
Walter Gropius
Sir Alec Guinness

H

Edith Hamilton
Learned Hand
W. C. Handy
Thomas Hardy
Rex Harrison
Helen Hayes
William Randolph
    Hearst
Katharine Hepburn
Hermann Hesse
Alfred Hitchcock
Thomas Hobbes
Laura Z. Hobson
Eric Hoffer

Hans Hofmann
Oliver Wendell Holmes
Oliver W. Holmes, Jr.
Herbert Clark Hoover
Bob Hope
Edgar Watson Howe
William Dean Howells
Charles Evans Hughes
Victor Hugo
Sol Hurok

I

William Ralph Inge

J

Thomas Jefferson
Lady Bird Johnson
Philip Johnson
Mother Jones
Carl Gustav Jung

K

Garson Kanin
Yousef Karsh
Helen Keller
Charles F. Kettering
Jiddu Krishnamurti
Maggie Kuhn
Stanley Kunitz

L

Dorothea Lange
Suzanne K. Langer
Eva Le Gallienne
Ninon de Lenclos
John L. Lewis
Anne Morrow
   Lindbergh
Walter Lippmann
Anita Loos
Clare Booth Luce

M

Douglas MacArthur
Sir Compton
   Mackenzie
Archibald MacLeish
Harold Macmillan
Golo Mann
Thomas Mann
Marya Mannes
Mao Zedong
Thurgood Marshall
Groucho Marx
John Masefield
Henri Matisse
W. Somerset Maugham
André Maurois
Elsa Maxwell
Barbara McClintock
Alexander Meiklejohn
Golda Meir
Dr. Karl Meninger
Robert Menzies

Michelangelo
James Michener
Henry Miller
Mistinguett
Claude Monet
Maria Montessori
Pierre Monteux
George Moore
Henry Moore
Samuel Eliot Morison
John, Lord Morley
Grandma Moses
Malcolm Muggeridge
Dr. Margaret Murray

N

Louise Nevelson
Cardinal John Henry
   Newman
Pat Nixon
Richard M. Nixon

O

Sean O'Casey
Georgia O'Keeffe
Sir Laurence Olivier

P

Linus Pauling
Ivan P. Pavlov
Norman Vincent Peale
Claude Pepper
Pablo Picasso
Mary Pickford
Max Planck
Plato
George W. Plunkett
Sir Karl Popper
Katherine Ann Porter
Anthony Powell
J. B. Priestley
V. S. Pritchett

R

Jeanette Rankin
Ronald Reagan
Theodor Reik
Agnes Repplier
James Reston
Jean Rhys
George Hyman
   Rickover
John D. Rockefeller
John D. Rockefeller, Jr.
Norman Rockwell
Ginger Rogers
Helena Rubenstein
Arthur Rubinstein
Bertrand Russell

S

Camille Saint-Saëns
Carl Sandburg

George Santayana
May Sarton
Elsa Schiaparelli
Albert Schweitzer
Florida Scott-Maxwell
George Bernard Shaw
Bishop Fulton Sheen
Jean Sibelius
Georges Simenon
Isaac Bashevis Singer
B. F. Skinner
Logan Pearsall Smith
Margaret Chase Smith
Dr. Benjamin Spock
Elizabeth Cady Stanton
Freya Stark
Wallace Stegner
Edward Steichen
Jimmy Stewart
I. F. Stone
Harriet Beecher Stowe

Igor Stravinsky
Albert Szent-Györgyi

Louis Untermeyer

V

Giuseppe Verdi
Elizabeth Gray Vining
François Marie de
    Voltaire

T

Jessica Tandy
Edward Teller
Alfred, Lord Tennyson
Mother Teresa
Dr. Lewis Thomas
Lowell Thomas
Norman Thomas
Dame Sybil Thorndike
Josef Broz Tito
J. R. R. Tolkien
Leo Tolstoy
Arnold J. Toynbee
Ben Travers
Bess Truman
Harry S. Truman

W

Izaak Walton
Sylvia Townsend
    Warner
Earl Warren
Noah Webster
Duke of Wellington
Eudora Welty
John Wesley
Jessamyn West

Mae West

Dame Rebecca West

John Hall Wheelock

E. B. White

Alfred North
  Whitehead

Billy Wilder

Walter Winchell

P. G. Wodehouse

Frank Lloyd Wright

Y

Edward Young

Z

Adolph Zukor

FOREWORD

by WALTER M. BORTZ II, M. D.

This book is the harvest of an elegant selection of writings by men and women who have lived long and seen much. Collectively they show that aging can and should be a good-news story. They help all of us learn what our whole lives might be. Aging is a self-fulfilling prophecy, and the old are the prophets. As the 80-year-old said to the youth, "I have the advantage over you because I know how it feels to be young, but you cannot know what it is like to be old." The old have survived. They nurture all of us. Wisdom derives from experience, and age has its advantages. We need to rediscover and respect them.

We have been given a good look at the first

two parts of life. Youth and adulthood have been very thoroughly mapped. But the third age of life, old age, appears through a gauzy haze of misunderstanding, stereotype, and fear. Almost all of the news about aging has been bad—and most of it has been *wrong*. The main reason is that throughout history we have died too soon! Just 90 years ago the average life expectancy in the United States was 45 years. It is still that, and even less, in many parts of the world.

Now, armed with an avalanche of scientific and medical data, we know that genetically we are designed to live 100-plus years. It is disuse and disease that are disabling and killing us early in our 60s, 70s, and 80s. We are finally recognizing that the increasing frailty of physical, psychological, and intellectual abilities with age is due mainly to processes that are preventable and reversible. They are not due to the effect of time on the human body. Because of this new information we are learning that the last of life should be the *best*—not the worst. Earlier emphasis on decline and loss has been shown to be wrong. For the first time we are individually and collectively given the precious task of redefining human aging. In our search for new definitions we look to those who have lived long. The people represented in this book are examples of productive old age. They show us how it should be done.

Joan Erickson observed, "Lots of old people don't become wise, but you don't get wise unless you age." Wisdom is the result of spending countless days and nights as a deep-well digger.

Who are the deep-well diggers of the world? What are the characteristics that propel these elite persons to positions that the rest of us admire and draw strength from? To find the answers we turn back in history and see that in all prior cultures respect and dignity were accorded the older members of the tribal community: the chief, headman, or members of the council of elders. The old, those closest to spiritual unity, were the keepers of the flame, the healers, the judges. Knowledge, understanding, and wisdom were the sources of high social rank. Tribal wisdom generally resided in the elders. They were the ones who had lived through the dry seasons and the wet, the hot years and the cold, pestilence and epidemics. They had learned how to give order to the chaos of nature because they had the longest time to practice. In every civilization the old were the archives, the living history books.

Hundreds of generations have gone since our days as simple hunters and gatherers. As we live longer now, we inherit the responsibility to transmit our knowledge. Age creates the responsibility that accompanies wisdom. Victor Borge once remarked that as he ages he sees more because time seems to have slowed down. Obviously, experience creates the ability to see more.

It is said that each of us is dealt a hand at the beginning of our lives and the cards determine our destiny. But one cannot ignore the element of cause and effect that we are able to interject. This book is filled with the thoughts of men and women who had a passion and made it happen. They chose not to let age slow them down. Their insights and searchings for meaning are preserved and extended to us. They help us manage our world. As the complexity of our modern lives increases and accepted social roles continue to change, our search for a new definition and meaning of aging intensifies, and the question we must ask ourselves is this: "Are the old to be a continuing resource or a liability?"

This book will acquaint or reacquaint us with, and give a better understanding of, a very special group of people who have lived long and productive lives. It is a collection of upbeat, often humorous, and concise thoughts of very famous and not-so-well-known people who have in common the fact that their lives cover a period of 80 years or more.

In their later years, they were perhaps bright enough, perhaps lucky enough, to fasten onto a life's ambition that gave them something to wake up for every morning. That momentum is what distinguishes the very special group of people featured here. It is what *Older and Wiser* is all about.

These men and women who lived rich, full lives into their eighth, ninth, and tenth decades should be a road map for us all. But unfortunately, because of its current preoccupation with youth, modern society distorts our perception of older people. The concept of mandatory retirement, for instance, is absurd. To establish that someone is all used up, that the best years are suddenly over at 65, rings a premature death knell for millions of us. How can we expect to remain keen and passionate in our later years when we are summarily removed from a critical life role? It is a sorry indication of our society's view of older people.

I recently gave a talk to a large audience, and when I was finished a gentleman approached and thanked me for saving his life. Puzzled, I asked him what he meant, and he told me that at age 82 he was alone, his wife and friends dead. He told me he no longer worked, his interests had dwindled, he felt depressed and unnecessary. He said he had been sitting at home, waiting for the hearse to pull up, but that he had come today to hear my talk and he realized it wasn't time yet.

The material in this book allows us to enjoy the harvest of many people of age. Their search for meaning has diverse origins and perspectives. But their messages to us show the careful burnishing that time alone can provide. Wisdom is the child of accumulated experience. Let us read about it and learn.

PREFACE

For this anthology we have collected little gems of wisdom from great people who lived fruitfully and productively in their later years. Their names and achievements may be familiar, but we may know very little about their intimate thoughts, especially on the subject of living and aging. This is the first collection in which famous oldsters reveal much of themselves in statements made late in life, and we hope this book will provide an original perspective from which to see and enjoy the wit and wisdom of some particularly fascinating contemporary and historical characters. Especially we wanted to show how mentally acute people continue to be in their old age. As it was necessary to draw an arbitrary age line somewhere, we limited our selection of quotes to those produced by our contributors when they were 60 years of age or more. All of those who grace our pages lived to (or currently are) at least 80 years of age.

As for how we derived the ages at which our contributors made certain statements, there were instances in which our sources specifically documented the year. In most cases, however, we determined the age by noting the year in which the author's work was published, and roughly calculating the author's age based on that date. In other instances, we were happy to encounter dated letters, speeches, anniversaries, or birthday celebrations.

Each author brings a different perspective to this project. In Gretchen's words, "I have always enjoyed the company of older people, admiring and appreciating their wisdom and experience. I find myself most intrigued by my older friends who have chosen to remain engaged in life, who remain vital and interested when many of their peers have opted to surrender. I find myself drawn toward their quiet, powerful courage.

"From my experiences with these special friends I am impressed by the notion that we all, young and old, have choices. I have learned that the final years can be fine and full. I have learned to be unafraid of wrinkled skin and gray hair. Fear is one of the biggest contributors to the myth of negative aging. Fear comes from the unknown. My brave old friends have teamed up with new friends I have found in this book, and together they give us the opportunity to look into the unknown and leave the fear where it belongs: behind us."

In Betty's words, "What started me on this book were quotes that I had collected for the past half-century. The early ones were poems and bits of famous books and plays that I had been required to memorize at school. Then they were romantic in nature and, in my "mature" years when I tried to resolve personal problems, I looked for answers in literature.

"Most recently I had a research job that included quotations, and finally, after reading Dr. Bortz's book on aging, I asked if I could help him on his next project. Somehow the subject of quotations came up, and I sent him samples from my collection. Subsequently, he introduced me to his daughter, Gretchen, and we began our three-year collaboration on this book."

We selected Walter M. Bortz II, M.D. to write the Foreword. He is one of America's most respected and acclaimed authorities on aging and is author of the best-selling book *We Live Too Short and Die Too Long* (Bantam, 1991). His belief that 120 years is a possible life-span and his DARE (Diet, Attitude, Rest, and Exercise) theory of how to achieve it helped inspire us to find out more about notables who lived effectively to a ripe old age.

Our continuous guidance and encouragement, and the final downsizing to eliminate all but the best quotes, were provided by our excellent editor, Elizabeth Zack.

We hope that after reading *Older and Wiser*, you too will recognize and be enthusiastic about how fulfilling the later years of one's life can be.

OLDER
AND
WISER

GOODMAN ACE ▪ 1899-1982

Actor called "America's greatest wit." He created and acted in the popular radio series "Easy Aces."

AT AGE 69, COMMENTING ABOUT BEING A SEXAGENARIAN:

"I like that word. It has a ring to it. A ring of excitement and élan. And, alas, of promise."

ROY ACUFF ▪ 1903-1993

U.S. country-and-western entertainer and record company executive. He was known as the "King of Country Music."

AT AGE 79:

"I'm going to be eighty soon, and I guess the one thing that puzzles me most is how quick it got here."

Ansel Adams ▪ 1902-1984

U.S. landscape photographer and conservationist. His works captured the beauty of such natural wonders as Yosemite National Park and Big Sur.

At age 82:

"If one feels inclined to embark on a journey into memory after 82 years, the experience promises to be kaleidoscopic and, perhaps, wilfully colored."

"Literally thousands of wonderful friends have accompanied me in life, and many now await me in the secret eternity to come. I have enjoyed the long voyage."

"In wisdom gathered over time I have found that every experience is a form of exploration."

"The only things in my life that compatibly exist with this grand universe are the creative works of the human spirit."

Henry Brooks Adams ▪ 1838-1918

U.S. historian, teacher, novelist, and grandson of John Adams.

REGARDING OLD AGE:

"The Indian summer of life should be a little sunny and a little sad, like the season, infinite in wealth and depth of tone—but never hustled."

AT AGE 68:

"A teacher affects eternity; he can never tell where his influence stops."

"A friend in power is a friend lost."

AT AGE 70:

"All experience is an arch to build upon."

John Quincy Adams ▪ 1767-1848

Sixth U.S. president and the only one whose father had also been president.

REGARDING OLD AGE:

"Old minds are like old horses; you must exercise them if you wish to keep them in working order."

AT AGE 79, ON THE ESTABLISHMENT OF THE SMITHSONIAN INSTITUTION:

"To furnish the means of acquiring knowledge is the greatest benefit that can be conferred upon mankind. It prolongs life itself and enlarges the sphere of human existence."

DURING HIS LAST ILLNESS:

"I inhabit a weak, frail, decayed tenement, battered by the winds and broken in on by the storms, and, from all I can learn, the landlord does not intend to repair."

MORTIMER ADLER ▪ 1902-

American author, teacher of the philosophy of law, and director of the Institute for Philosophical Research. In 1944 he created the Great Books program.

REGARDING AGING:

"The purpose of learning is growth, and our minds, unlike our bodies, can continue growing as we continue to live."

Eddie Albert ▪ 1908-

U.S. actor who, after being in 60 films, is an active environmentalist.

At age 83:

> **"Just about the time a man grows up to really lock horns with this fantastic civilization, we tell him to go to sleep. The stupidity and injustice of throwing that experience down the drain just enrages me."**

> **"Today our complicated society requires experienced judgment calls, and that experience only comes with years on the firing line."**

(Amos) Bronson Alcott ▪
1799-1888

U.S. educational reformer and transcendental philosopher known for his wry satire. The father of Louisa May Alcott, he founded Boston's famous Trinity School.

REGARDING OLD AGE:

"When one finds company in himself and his pursuits, he cannot feel old, no matter what his years may be."

AT AGE 78:

"That is a good book which is opened with expectation and closed with delight and profit."

AT AGE 89:

"To be ignorant of one's ignorance is the malady of the ignorant."

"One must be a wise reader to quote wisely and well."

SIR HARDY AMIES • 1909-

British tailor, and dressmaker to Queen Elizabeth II.

AT AGE 80:

"The best-dressed woman is one whose clothes wouldn't look too strange in the country."

MARIAN ANDERSON • 1902-1993

U.S. concert artist. The first black to perform in a major role at the Metropolitan Opera, she was the U.S. delegate to the U.N. in 1955.

AT AGE 63:

"You lose a lot of time hating people."

JAMES B. ANGELL ▪ 1829-1916

American educator, editor, and diplomat. For 38 years he was the president of the University of Michigan.

REGARDING HIS SECRET TO A SUCCESSFUL OLD AGE:

"Grow antennae, not horns."

WALTER ANNENBERG ▪ 1908-

U.S. publisher and philanthropist. His art collection rivals that of most museums.

AT AGE 85, ON GIVING $365 MILLION TO FOUR SCHOOLS:

"For every advantage you have a corresponding responsibility."

"I'm interested in the young people because the character of our country will be shaped by young people in the days ahead."

Susan B. Anthony ▪ 1820-1906

U.S. social reformer and pioneer. A propagandist for women's suffrage, she was elected to the Hall of Fame for Great Americans 44 years after her death.

From age 48 until her death at 86, this was the caption printed on the front page of her newspaper, *Revolution*:

> **"The true Republic: men their rights and nothing more; women their rights and nothing less."**

At age 77:

> **"There never will be complete equality until women themselves help to make laws and elect lawmakers."**

Elizabeth Arden ▪ 1878-1966

U.S. cosmetics executive. The founder and sole owner of Elizabeth Arden, Inc., she was at her death one of the richest women in the world.

REGARDING OLD AGE:

"I'm not interested in age. People who tell their age are silly. You're as old as you feel."

Fred Astaire ▪ 1899-1987

Leading American dance star of his generation; also an actor and singer. With his sister Adele he formed a successful Broadway team. After his sister retired, he became a film actor. He was still working in his 80s.

REGARDING OLD AGE:

"Old age is like everything else. To make a success of it, you've got to start young."

Brooke Astor ▪ 1902-

Unofficial First Lady of New York City. She is a matron of society and philanthropy.

At age 80:

> **"Mirrors in a room, water in a landscape, eyes in a face—those are what give character."**

At age 89, when planning a party to celebrate her 90th birthday:

> **"And there'll be dancing! I, for one, intend to dance till dawn."**

MARY ASTOR ▪ 1906-1987

American actress. A leading lady in many films of the 1920s, 1930s, and 1940s.

AT AGE 61:

> **"It's not good to take sentimental journeys. You see the differences instead of the samenesses."**

> **"A painter paints, a musician plays, a writer writes—but a movie actor waits."**

LADY NANCY ASTOR ▪ 1879-1964

Viscountess and politician. In 1919 she became the first woman to take a seat in the British House of Commons. She was devoted to the causes of temperance and reforms in women's and children's welfare.

AT AGE 80:

"I used to dread getting older because I thought I would not be able to do all the things I wanted to do, but now that I am older, I find that I don't want to do them."

GERTRUDE ATHERTON ▪ 1857-1948

American author and great-grandniece of Benjamin Franklin.

AT AGE 88:

"Women love the lie that saves their pride, but never the unflattering truth."

CLEMENT ATTLEE ▪ 1883–1967

British statesman and lawyer. During World War II he served on Winston Churchill's cabinet and later became prime minister.

AT AGE 74:

> **"Democracy means government by discussion, but it is only effective if you can stop people talking."**

ENID BAGNOLD ▪ 1889–1981

English novelist and playwright.

AT AGE 80:

> **"When I look back on the pain of sex . . . and contrast it with affection of two people who have lived a life together, it's the affection I find richer. It's that I would have again."**

> **"As for death, one gets used to it, even if it's only other people's death that you get used to."**

John Bardeen ▪ 1908-1991

American physicist and electrical engineer who shared two Nobel Prizes in Physics, first for inventing the transistor, which made contemporary miniaturized electronics possible (1956), and later for his work on medical diagnostic procedures (1972).

At age 64, when he received his second Nobel Prize:

> **"I'd say you have to believe in persistence. It sometimes pays off."**

NATALIE CLIFFORD BARNEY ▪
1876-1972

French author.

> **"If we keep an open mind, too much is likely to fall into it."**

> **"The advantage of love at first sight is that it delays a second sight."**

> **"Why grab possessions like thieves, or divide them like socialists, when you can ignore them like wise men?"**

> **"Youth is not a question of years; one is young or old from birth."**

ETHEL BARRYMORE ▪ 1879-1959

American actress and sister to Lionel and John Barrymore. From 1900 to 1940 she was called "the First Lady of the American Theater."

AT AGE 74:

"For an actress to be a success she must have the face of Venus, the brains of Minerva, the grace of Terpsichore, the memory of Macaulay, the figure of Juno, and the hide of a rhinoceros."

AT AGE 76:

"You must learn day by day, year by year, to broaden your horizon. The more things you love, the more you are interested in, the more you enjoy, the more you are indignant about—the more you have left when anything happens."

BERNARD BARUCH ▪ 1870-1965

U.S. elder statesman and economic adviser to presidents.

REGARDING OLD AGE:

"There's only one thing wrong with the younger generation—a lot of us don't belong to it anymore."

"Age is only a number, a cipher for the records. A man can't retire his experience. He must use it."

AT AGE 85:

"I will never be an old man. To me, old age is always 15 years older than I am."

AT AGE 87:

"During my 87 years I have witnessed a whole succession of technological revolutions; but none of them has done away with the need for character in the individual, or the ability to think."

JAMES BEARD ▪ 1903-1985

U.S. cookbook author and chef.

AT AGE 80:

"I don't like gourmet cooking, or 'this' cooking, or 'that' cooking. I like good cooking."

LORD WILLIAM BEAVERBROOK ▪ 1879-1964

British newspaper publisher, politician, statesman, and financier.

AT AGE 75:

"I suppose I will go on selling newspapers until at last will come the late night final."

Sir Thomas Beecham ▪ 1879-1961

English conductor who organized the London Philharmonic Orchestra. He was knighted in 1915.

AT AGE 76:

"If an opera cannot be played by an organ-grinder—as Puccini's and Verdi's melodies were played—it is not going to achieve immortality."

Sir Max Beerbohm ▪ 1872-1956

English essayist, caricaturist, and drama critic.

ABOUT HIS OWN AGING:

"I should like everyone to go about doing just as he pleased—short of altering any of the things to which I have grown accustomed."

Melvin Belli ▪ 1907-

Flamboyant U.S. attorney.

At age 74:

"There is never a deed so foul that something couldn't be said for the guy; that's why there are lawyers."

David Ben-Gurion ▪ 1886-1973

The first prime minister of Israel, often called "Father of the Nation."

At age 70:

"In Israel, in order to be a realist, you must believe in miracles."

Jack Benny ▪ 1894-1974

Deadpan American comedian known for his brilliant timing. His radio and TV career spanned three decades.

About aging:

> **"I don't deserve this award, but I have arthritis and I don't deserve that either."**

> **"Mary and I have been married 47 years and not once have we had an argument serious enough to mention the word divorce—murder, yes, but divorce, never."**

BERNARD BERENSON ▪ 1865-1959

American art critic and an authority on Italian Renaissance art.

ABOUT LIFE:

> **"Life has taught me that it is not for our faults that we are disliked and even hated, but for our qualities."**

AT AGE 82:

> **"Time flies swifter and ever swifter. I daresay if I live long enough, perhaps another 20 years, time may cease to exist for me."**

> **"There is a certain sweetness in being what one is now . . . so appreciative, so enjoying, so grateful for what has been, and for what is now. It means something to be able to rise above aches and pains, and inertias, and to glory in the world. . . ."**

Irving Berlin ▪ 1888-1989

Composer of musicals and more than 1,000 songs. Born in Temun, Russia, he came to the U.S. at age four. He played piano in one key—F-sharp—and never learned to read or transcribe music. He received the Congressional Gold Medal for his song "God Bless America."

At age 70:

> **"The toughest thing about success is that you've got to keep on being a success. Talent is only a starting point in this business. You've got to keep on working that talent."**

EUBIE BLAKE ▪ 1883-1983

American ragtime jazz composer, pianist, and pioneer of boogie-woogie.

AT AGE 100:

"Those docs, they always ask you how you live so long. I tell 'em: 'If I'd known I was gonna live this long, I'd have taken better care of myself.' "

DANIEL BOONE ▪ 1734-1820

American frontiersman and explorer.

IN HIS 80S, WHEN ASKED IF HE HAD EVER BEEN LOST:

"No, I can't say I was ever lost, but I was bewildered once for three days."

Daniel J. Boorstin ▪ 1914-

U.S. historian, director of the Smithsonian Institution's Museum of History and Technology, and Librarian of Congress.

AT AGE 61:

"The most important American addition to the World Experience was the simple surprising fact of America. We have helped prepare mankind for all its later surprises."

AT AGE 62:

"The American experience stirred mankind from discovery to exploration, from the cautious quest for what they knew (or thought they knew) was out there, to an enthusiastic reaching to the unknown."

WILLIAM BOOTH ▪ 1829-1912

English evangelist and founder of the Salvation Army.

AT AGE 61:

"**Many a man takes to beer, not from the love of beer, but from a natural craving for the light, warmth, company, and comfort which is thrown in along with the beer, and which he cannot get except by buying beer.**"

VICTOR BORGE ▪ 1909-

Danish-American concert pianist turned comedic piano player.

AT AGE 75:

> "Humor is something that thrives between man's aspirations and his limitations. There is more logic in humor than in anything else. Because, you see, humor is truth."

AT AGE 85:

> "I'm celebrating my 75th birthday, which is sort of embarrassing because I'm 85."

Jorge Luis Borges • 1899-1986

Argentine poet, critic, and master of the short story. During his life he was widely acclaimed as the foremost contemporary South-American writer.

AT AGE 65:

"The flattery of posterity is not worth much more than contemporary flattery, which is worth nothing."

"I cannot walk through the suburbs in the solitude of the night without thinking that the night pleases us because it suppresses idle details, just as our memory does."

AT AGE 73:

"Writing is nothing more than a guided dream."

Omar Bradley ▪ 1893-1981

The last U.S. five-star general. Known affectionately by his troops as "the GI's General," he was World War II commander in North Africa, Sicily, and the Normandy Invasion.

AT AGE 66:

> **"I am convinced that the best service a retired general can perform is to turn in his tongue along with his suit, and to mothball his opinions."**

AT AGE 67:

> **"Bravery is the capacity to perform properly even when scared half to death."**

LOUIS D. BRANDEIS ▪ 1856-1941

U.S. jurist, lawyer, and associate justice of the Supreme Court from 1916 until his retirement at age 82.

AT AGE 64:

"In frank expression of conflicting opinion lies the greatest promise of wisdom in governmental action."

AT AGE 72:

"Crime is contagious. It breeds contempt for law."

AT AGE 76:

"If we would guide by the light of reason, we must let our minds be bold."

WILLIAM J. BRENNAN ▪ 1906-

U.S. Supreme Court justice.

AT AGE 79:

"We current justices read the Constitution in the only way that we can, as 20th-century Americans. The ultimate question must be, What do the words of the text mean in our time?"

PEARL BUCK ▪ 1892-1973

American author who lived in China for 10 years as a missionary. She received the Pulitzer Prize in Fiction for *The Good Earth* and the Nobel Prize in Literature.

AT AGE 62:

"Somehow our society must make it right and possible for old people not to fear the young or be deserted by them, for the test of a civilization is the way it cares for its helpless members."

At age 67:

"Inside myself is a place where I live all alone, and that's where you renew your springs that never dry up."

At age 75:

"Praise out of season, or tactlessly bestowed, can freeze the heart as much as blame."

At age 79:

"Ah, perhaps one has to be very old before one learns how to be amused rather than shocked."

Luis Buñuel ▪ 1900-1983

Spanish film director. He joined Dali to make some early surrealistic films.

AT AGE 83:

"The bar . . . is an exercise in solitude. Above all else, it must be quiet, dark, very comfortable—and, contrary to modern mores, no music of any kind, no matter how faint."

"God and Country are an unbeatable team; they break all records for oppression and bloodshed."

"If the devil were to offer me a resurgence of what is commonly called virility, I'd decline. 'Just keep my liver and lungs in good working order,' I'd reply, 'so I can go on drinking and smoking.' "

George Burns ▪ 1896-

U.S. comedian/actor who, at 80, was the oldest person ever to win an Oscar.

AT AGE 80:

"I think the only reason you should retire is if you can find something you enjoy more than what you're doing now."

AT AGE 82:

"If it's a good script I'll do it. And if it's a bad script and they pay me enough, I'll do it."

AT AGE 83:

"Too bad that all the people who know how to run the country are busy driving taxicabs and cutting hair."

"The most important thing in acting is honesty. If you can fake that, you've got it made."

"Happiness? A good cigar and a good meal, a good cigar and a good woman— or a bad woman—it depends how much happiness you can handle."

REGARDING OLD AGE:

"I don't believe in dying. It's been done. I'm working on a new exit. Besides, I can't die now—I'm booked."

"You know you're getting old when you stoop to tie your shoes and wonder what else you can do when you're down there."

"If you live to the age of 100 you have it made, because very few people die past the age of 100."

JOHN BURROUGHS ▪ 1837-1921

U.S. newspaper reporter, bank examiner, treasury clerk, author, and naturalist.

AT AGE 63:

> **"It is always easier to believe than to deny. Our minds are naturally affirmative."**

AT AGE 65:

> **"Time does not become sacred to us until we have lived it, until it has passed over us and taken with it part of ourselves."**

AT AGE 73:

> **"Joy in the universe, and keen curiosity about it all—that has been my religion."**

WILLIAM BURROUGHS ▪ 1914-

American novelist.

AT AGE 71:

> "After one look at this planet, any visitor from outer space would say, 'I WANT TO SEE THE MANAGER.'"

AT AGE 73:

> "So cheat your landlord if you can and must, but do not try to shortchange the Muse. It cannot be done. You can't fake quality any more than you can fake a good meal."

> "Desperation is the raw material of drastic change. Only those who can leave behind everything they have ever believed in can hope to escape."

AT AGE 78:

> "Happiness is a by-product of function. You are happy when you are functioning."

Vannevar Bush ▪ 1890-1974

U.S. electrical engineer and physicist. During World War II he led the U.S. Office of Scientific Research and Development, directing such programs as the development of the first atomic bomb.

At age 77:

> **"Science has a simple faith that transcends utility. It is the faith that it is the privilege of man to learn to understand, and that this is his mission."**

JOHN CAGE ▪ 1912-1993

U.S. composer and musician. He is said to have had a greater impact on contemporary music than any other American composer in the 20th century.

AT AGE 80:

"**As I get older my interests multiply rather than lessen in number.**"

"**If you are self-employed, you will see each day as useful, no matter how old you are.**"

"**If you can enjoy the worst things, then the rest is easy.**"

Elias Canetti ▪ 1905-

Austrian novelist and philosopher.

AT AGE 71:

> **"One should use praise to recognize what one is not."**

> **"The self-explorer, whether he wants to or not, becomes an explorer of everything else."**

Thomas Carlyle ▪ 1795-1881

Scottish essayist and historian, and one of the brilliant literary masters of his era. He was influenced by Goethe and was a great friend of Emerson.

AT AGE 71:

"Talk that does not end in any kind of action is better suppressed altogether."

AT AGE 86:

"Under all speech that is good for anything there lies a silence that is better. Silence is deep as Eternity; speech is shallow as Time."

LILLIAN CARTER ▪ 1898-1983

The mother of U.S. President Jimmy Carter. Known fondly as "Miss Lillian," she joined the Peace Corps at age 68 and served as a nurse in India.

AT AGE 78:

> **"Every time I think that I'm getting old, and gradually going to the grave, something else happens."**

AT AGE 82:

> **"Sometimes when I look at my children, I say to myself: 'Lillian, you should have stayed a virgin.'"**

BARBARA CARTLAND ▪ 1901-

English novelist known as "the Queen of Romance" and one of the best-selling authors of all time. She writes Cinderella stories with happy endings.

AT AGE 73:

"I'll keep going till my face falls off."

AT AGE 75, ON THE PUBLICATION OF HER 217TH BOOK:

"As long as the plots keep arriving from outer space, I'll go on with my virgins."

AT AGE 83:

"France is the only place where you can make love in the afternoon without people hammering on your door."

Pablo Casals ▪ 1876-1973

Spanish master of the cello, conductor, composer, and pianist. He established the cello as a solo instrument and was still thrilling world audiences at 95.

Regarding old age:

"As long as one can admire and love, then one is young forever."

At age 93:

"If you continue to work and to absorb the beauty in the world around you, you will find that age does not necessarily mean getting old."

"The man who works and is never bored is never old. Work and interest in worthwhile things are the best remedy for age. Each day I am reborn. Each day I must begin again."

"I do not think a day passes in my life in which I fail to look with fresh amazement at the miracle of nature."

MARCUS PORCIUS CATO ▪ 234-149 B.C.

Roman statesman, soldier, and writer. He learned Greek in his 80s. He was the first significant Latin prose writer.

AT AGE 83:

"A man who is always living in the midst of his studies and labours does not perceive when old age creeps upon him."

Marc Chagall ▪ 1887-1985

Modern Russian artist who was still working in his 90s.

AT AGE 73:

"When I am finishing a picture I hold some God-made object next to it. If the painting stands up beside a thing man cannot make, the painting is authentic. If there is a clash between the two, it is bad art."

AT AGE 90:

"I work as long as I have strength. Without my work, my life would be idiotic."

"Only love interests me, and I am only in contact with things that revolve around love."

Coco Chanel ▪ 1883-1971

French designer who, at age 85, was still ruling her empire. She was responsible for the death of the corset and the birth of costume jewelry.

AT AGE 7 3:

> **"Nature gives you the face you have at 20; it is up to you to merit the face you have at 50."**

AT AGE 7 4:

> **"Fashion is made to become unfashionable."**

AT AGE 7 8:

> **"How many cares one loses when one decides not to be something, but to be someone."**

Charlie Chaplin ▪ 1889-1977

English film actor, king of silent-screen comedies, director, producer, writer, and composer. In 1975 he was knighted by Queen Elizabeth II.

AT AGE 75:

"All I need to make a comedy is a park, a policeman, and a pretty girl."

"The saddest thing I can imagine is to get used to luxury."

AT AGE 87:

"I don't believe that the public knows what it wants."

JOHN CHEEVER ▪ 1912-1982

U.S. novelist and short-story writer noted for his prize-winning fiction about suburbia.

AT AGE 66:

"Art is the triumph over chaos."

AT AGE 67:

"The need to write comes from the need to make sense of one's life and discover one's usefulness."

"I can't write without a reader. It's precisely like a kiss—you can't do it alone."

Maurice Chevalier ▪ 1888-1972

French entertainer whose trademarks were a charming manner and a straw hat.

At age 68:

"An artist carries on throughout his life a mysterious, uninterrupted conversation with his public."

At age 70:

"The French are true romantics. They feel the only difference between a man of 40 and one of 70 is 30 years' experience."

At age 72:

"Old age isn't so bad when you consider the alternative."

JULIA CHILD ▪ 1912-

American author and TV personality who brought the world of French cooking into American homes.

AT AGE 68:

"Too many cooks spoil the broth, but it takes only one to burn it."

AGATHA CHRISTIE ▪ 1890-1976

English detective novelist and playwright whose books have sold more than 100 million copies.

AT AGE 64, ABOUT HER HUSBAND:

"An archaeologist is the best husband any woman can have; the older she gets, the more interested he is in her."

AT AGE 75:

"I learned that one can never go back, that one should not ever try to go back— that the essence of life is going forward. Life is really a One Way Street."

SIR WINSTON CHURCHILL ▪
1874-1965

British soldier, statesman, journalist, historian, and orator. At 79 he was awarded the Nobel Prize in Literature for *The Second World War.* At 89 he became the first person in history to be awarded honorary U.S. citizenship.

REGARDING OLD AGE:

> **"We are happier in many ways when we are old than when we were young. The young sow wild oats. The old grow sage."**

AT AGE 68:

> **"The problems of victory are more agreeable than the problems of defeat, but they are no less difficult."**

AT AGE 74:

> **"The English never draw a line without blurring it."**

AT AGE 75:

"I am ready to meet my Maker. Whether my Maker is prepared for the great ordeal of meeting me is another matter."

AT AGE 78:

"Everyone has his day, and some days last longer than others."

AT AGE 79, ON ACCEPTING THE NOBEL PRIZE IN LITERATURE:

"I do hope you are right."

AT AGE 80:

"Without tradition, art is a flock of sheep without a shepherd. Without innovation, it is a corpse."

"A fanatic is one who can't change his mind and won't change the subject."

Paul Claudel ■ 1868-1955

French dramatist, poet, and ambassador to the United States.

AT AGE 61:

"When a man tries to imagine Paradise on earth, the immediate result is a very respectable Hell."

Georges Clemenceau ■ 1841-1929

French statesman who became premier of France and was highly regarded as an author.

AT AGE 78:

"It is far easier to make war than to make peace."

AT AGE 80, ON NOTICING A PRETTY GIRL ON THE CHAMPS ÉLYSÉES:

"Oh, to be 70 again."

AT AGE 87:

"A man's life is interesting when he has failed: It's a sign that he tried to surpass himself."

ELIZABETH COATSWORTH ▪
1893-1986

U.S. poet and author of short stories and books.

AT AGE 83:

> "Outwardly I am 83, but inwardly I am every age, with the emotions and experience of each period."

> "During much of my life I was anxious to be what someone else wanted me to be. Now I have given up that struggle. I am what I am."

> "Only of one thing I am sure: When I dream, I am always ageless."

COLETTE ▪ 1873-1954

French novelist known for her sharp witticisms.

AT AGE 60:

> **"Perhaps the only misplaced curiosity is that which persists in trying to find out here, on this side of death, what lies beyond the grave."**

> **"It is wise to apply the oil of refined politeness to the mechanism of friendship."**

REGARDING OLD AGE:

> **"What a wonderful life I've had! I only wish I'd realized it sooner."**

ALISTAIR COOKE ▪ 1908-

English-born U.S. journalist and host of TV's "Masterpiece Theatre."

AT AGE 60:

"All presidents start out to run a crusade but after a couple of years they find they are running something less heroic. The people are well cured by then of election fever during which they think they are choosing Moses. In the third year they look on the man as a sinner and a bumbler and begin to poke around for rumours of another Messiah."

AT AGE 65:

"Hollywood grew to be the most flourishing factory of popular mythology since the Greeks."

Lady Diana Cooper ▪ 1892-1986

English socialite.

Regarding aging:

"Age wins and one must learn to grow old. I must learn to walk this long unlovely wintry way, looking for spectacles, shunning the cruel looking-glass, laughing at my clumsiness, not expecting gallantry yet disappointed to receive none."

At age 86, upon hearing her name coupled with that of Sir Robert Mayer, who was almost 100 years old:

"My dear, when you are my age you will realize that what you need is a maturer man."

Aaron Copland • 1900-1990

U.S. composer called "the Dean of American Composers."

At age 76:

"You compose because you want to make some sort of permanent statement about the way it feels to live now, today. So that when it's all gone, people will be able to go to the artwork of the time and get a sense of what it felt like to be alive this year."

At age 80:

"So long as the human spirit thrives on this planet, music in some living form will accompany it and sustain it and give it expressive meaning."

LE CORBUSIER ▪ 1881-1965

French architect, city planner, designer, and educator.

AT AGE 80:

"I prefer drawing to talking. Drawing is faster, and leaves less room for lies."

KATHARINE CORNELL ▪ 1893-1974

U.S. stage actress.

IN HER 70S:

"When an actress is younger she likes to lower her age, but when she is older she likes to add to her years."

Norman Corwin ▪ 1910-

American author, radio producer and director, newspaper reporter and columnist.

AT AGE 81:

> **"I am aware there may be limited time for me. To the extent that there is less time, my need to create becomes sharper, keener."**

AT AGE 81, REGARDING SEX:

> **"Nobody should assume that when one has passed 80 interest in that department of life has eroded or disappeared."**

JACQUES COUSTEAU ▪ 1910-

French undersea explorer and author, famous for his movie and TV documentaries. In 1943 he invented the self-contained underwater breathing apparatus (scuba).

AT AGE 61:

"What is a scientist after all? It is a curious man looking through a keyhole, the keyhole of nature, trying to know what's going on."

Malcolm Cowley ▪ 1898-1989

American poet, essayist, and literary editor of *The New Republic*.

At age 80:

> **"The men and women I envy are those who accept old age as a series of challenges. For such persons, every new infirmity is an enemy to be outwitted, an obstacle to be overcome by force of will . . . and sometimes they win a major success."**

> **"To enter the country of old age is a new experience, different from what you supposed it to be. Nobody, man or woman, knows the country until he has lived in it and has taken out his citizenship papers."**

Hume Cronyn ▪ 1911-

Canadian character actor. He is best known for his stage appearances with his wife, Jessica Tandy.

At age 80:

"The lines, the wrinkles . . . let them get deeper, particularly the laugh lines. That's not only what gives life its savor, it's the thing that charges our batteries."

Imogen Cunningham ▪ 1883-1976

American photographer. Her career lasted for seven decades.

At age 87:

"Fame is what comes after you're dead. When you're alive it's notoriety—and an annoyance. I'm just a working woman."

In her 90s, when asked to state her religion on a hospital form:

"Haven't chosen yet."

SALVADOR DALI ▪ 1904-1989

Spanish painter and controversial figure in the international art world. He was a leader of Surrealism.

AT AGE 72:

> **"Drawing is the honesty of art. There is no possibility of cheating. It is either good or bad."**

AT AGE 76:

> **"Each morning when I awake, I experience again a supreme pleasure—that of being Salvador Dali."**

AT AGE 80, REPLYING TO REPORTS THAT HIS ASSISTANTS DID MUCH OF HIS PAINTINGS:

> **"Let my enemies devour each other."**

Clarence Darrow ▪ 1857-1938

American attorney. He gained fame as the defense attorney in the Scopes trial, which challenged the constitutionality of Tennessee's existing anti-evolution law.

At age 63:

"As long as the world shall last there will be wrongs, and if no man objected and no man rebelled, those wrongs would last forever."

At age 68:

"To think is to differ."

"I do not pretend to know where many ignorant men are sure—that is all agnosticism means."

> **"At 20 a man is full of fight and hope. He wants to reform the world. When he's 70 he still wants to reform the world, but he knows he can't."**

ROBERTSON DAVIES ▪ 1913-

Canadian novelist and journalist.

AT AGE 66:

> **"A truly great book should be read in youth, again in maturity and once more in old age, as a fine building should be seen by morning light, at noon and by moonlight."**

BETTE DAVIS ▪ 1908-1989

One of the foremost dramatic American actresses in film history. At age 72, she celebrated her 50th year in show business by appearing in her 85th film.

AT AGE 66:

> "Attempt the impossible in order to improve your work."

> "I survived because I was tougher than anybody else."

AT AGE 75:

> "I've never been a big churchgoer. Being a working woman, I decided God would allow me Sundays off."

AT AGE 77:

> "People often become actresses because of something they dislike about themselves: They pretend they are someone else."

CHARLES G. DAWES ▪ 1865-1951

American statesman, banker, vice-president, and ambassador to Great Britain. He was awarded the Nobel Peace Prize for developing the Dawes Plan to stabilize post-World War I finances.

AT AGE 66:

"American diplomacy is easy on the brain but hell on the feet."

DOROTHY DAY ▪ 1897-1980

U.S. reformer. A founder and head of the pacifist Catholic Movement, she was jailed numerous times in the 1950s for protests against preparations for nuclear war.

AT AGE 78:

"The best thing to do with the best things in life is to give them up."

Charles de Gaulle ▪ 1890-1970

French statesman, soldier, and writer. He was leader in exile of the French government during World War II, returning to his country as president at age 68 and remaining in office until he was 79.

AT AGE 72:

"How can you be expected to govern a country that has 246 kinds of cheese?"

AT AGE 73:

"Treaties are like roses and young girls. They last while they last."

AT AGE 75:

"To govern is always to choose among disadvantages."

AT AGE 76:

"I respect only those who resist me, but I cannot tolerate them."

AGNES DE MILLE ▪ 1905-1993

American choreographer and dancer. Influenced by the work of Martha Graham, she brought ballet to musical comedy.

AT AGE 67:

"The truest expression of a people is in its dances and its music. Bodies never lie."

HELENE DEUTSCH ▪ 1884-1982

U.S. psychoanalyst, a pioneer of the Freudian movement, and last of the original Freudians.

AT AGE 89:

"The embattled gates to equal rights indeed opened up for modern women, but I sometimes think to myself: 'That's not what I meant by freedom—it is only social progress.' "

JOHN DEWEY ▪ 1859-1952

U.S. philosopher, educator, and author. The foremost authority on progressive education, he taught at Columbia University until 1930. At the age of 90 he published his last book.

AT AGE 61:

"Intelligence is in constant process of forming, and its retention requires constant alertness in observing consequences, an open-minded will to learn, and courage in readjustment."

AT AGE 70:

"Every great advancement in science has issued from a new audacity of imagination."

MARLENE DIETRICH ▪ 1901-1992

Film actress born in Germany, she came to the U.S. in 1930.

AT AGE 60, REGARDING OLD PEOPLE:

"I love them, because it is a joy to find thoughts one might have beautifully expressed with much authority by someone recognizedly wiser than oneself."

"Once a woman has forgiven her man, she must not reheat his sins for breakfast."

"Grumbling is the death of love."

U.S. newspaper reporter who covered many sensational murder cases, and columnist who gave advice to the lovelorn.

AT AGE 65:

> **"I have learned to live each day as it comes, and not borrow trouble by dreading tomorrow. It is the dark menace of the future that makes cowards of us."**

> **"So many persons who think divorce is a panacea for every ill find out, when they try it, that the remedy is worse than the disease."**

WILLIAM O. DOUGLAS ▪ 1898-1980

American jurist, world traveler, conservationist, outdoorsman, and author. He served 36 years on the U.S. Supreme Court—longer than any other justice to date.

AT AGE 72:

"Where there is a persistent sense of futility, there is violence, and that is where we are today."

W. E. B. DUBOIS ▪ 1868-1963

American educator, author, and civil rights leader. He founded the NAACP in 1909 and joined the Communist Party in 1961, thereafter renouncing his U.S. citizenship and moving to Ghana.

AT AGE 63:

"If the unemployed could eat plans and promises they would be able to spend the winter on the Riviera."

Marcel Duchamp ▪ 1887-1968

French-American painter. An important Cubist and founder of Dadaism, he gave up painting at age 35 in favor of chess.

AT AGE 63:

"Unless a picture shocks, it is nothing."

Will Durant ▪ 1885-1981

American historian, essayist, and critic of popular philosophy and history. He collaborated with his wife, Ariel, for 30 years on *The Story of Civilization*, a monumental work stretching from prehistory to the 18th century.

REMEMBERING HIS YOUTH:

"Sixty years ago I knew everything; now I know nothing; education is a progressive discovery of our own ignorance."

At age 73:

"Nothing is often a good thing to do, and always a clever thing to say."

At age 78:

"Civilization is a stream with banks. The stream is filled with the things historians usually record, while on the banks, unnoticed, people build homes, make love, and raise children. The story of civilization is the story of what happened on the banks."

At age 90:

"The love we have in our youth is superficial compared to the love that an old man has for his old wife."

Marguerite Duras ■ 1914-

French author and filmmaker.

At Age 73:

"You have to be very fond of men. Very, very fond. You have to be very fond of them to love them. Otherwise they are simply unbearable."

"Whether you're a man or a woman, the fascination resides in finding out that we're alike."

"The best way to fill time is to waste it."

RICHARD EBERHART ▪ 1904-

American poet who often writes about growing old. He was U.S. Poet Laureate in 1987.

AT AGE 85:

> **"I would no more quarrel with a man because of his religion than I would because of his art."**

THOMAS ALVA EDISON ▪ 1847-1931

American inventor. Among his first inventions were the transmitter and receiver for the automatic telegraph. He also invented the first electric light bulb, and his phonograph was the first instrument of its kind.

AT AGE 68:

> **"I'm proud of the fact that I never invented weapons to kill."**

AT AGE 84:

> **"I am long on ideas, but short on time. I only expect to live to be about 100."**

CHARLES WILLIAM ELIOT ▪ 1834-1926

American educator and president of Harvard University for 40 years.

AT AGE 70, ON WHY HE WANTED TO DROP BASEBALL AS A COLLEGE SPORT:

"I understand that a curve ball is thrown with a deliberate attempt to deceive. Surely that is not an ability we should want to foster at Harvard."

QUEEN MOTHER ELIZABETH ▪ 1900-

Consort of George VI of Great Britain. Known as "Queen Mum," she remains one of the best-loved figures in the British royal family.

IN HER 80s, WHEN CECIL BEATON OFFERED TO RETOUCH THE WRINKLES IN A PHOTOGRAPH OF HER:

"I would not want it to be thought that I had lived for all these years without having anything to show for it."

HAVELOCK ELLIS ▪ 1859-1939

English psychologist and author. A pioneer writer on the psychology of sex, he conducted the first study of homosexuality.

AT AGE 63:

"All civilization has from time to time become a thin crust over a volcano of revolution."

AT AGE 64:

"A man must not swallow more beliefs than he can digest."

"The sun, the moon and the stars would have disappeared long ago . . . had they happened to be within the reach of predatory human hands."

Sam Ervin ▪ 1896-1985

U.S. politician, lawyer, and senator from North Carolina (1954-75). At age 76 he headed the Senate Select Committee investigating the Watergate scandal.

AT AGE 77, DURING THE WATERGATE HEARINGS:

"I'm not going to let anybody whisper something in my ear that no one else can hear. That is not executive privilege; it is poppycock."

AT AGE 85:

"Humor is one of God's most marvelous gifts. Humor gives us smiles, laughter, and gaiety. Humor reveals the roses and hides the thorns. Humor makes our heavy burdens light and smooths the rough spots in our pathways. Humor endows us with the capacity to clarify the obscure, to simplify the complex, to deflate the pompous, to chastise the arrogant, to point a moral, and to adorn a tale."

Dame Edith Evans · 1888-1976

English actress celebrated for her Shake-spearean performances. She made her first film when she was 60, and at 87 she acted and sang the Dowager Queen in a musical version of *Cinderella*.

Regarding the process of aging:

"Life is long enough but not quite broad enough. Things crowd in so thickly and it takes time for experience to become clarified."

At age 68:

"When a woman behaves like a man, why doesn't she behave like a nice man?"

Clifton Fadiman ▪ 1904-

American essayist, author, and radio performer.

AT AGE 73:

"A sense of humor . . . is the ability to understand a joke—and that the joke is oneself."

Millicent Fenwick ▪ 1910-

American politician and editor. From age 65 to age 72 she was a member of the House of Representatives (1975-1982).

AT AGE 71:

"When you're old, everything you do is sort of a miracle."

AT AGE 72:

"A politician should be able to look anyone in the eye and say: 'Sorry, I can't do that.'"

James E. "Sunny Jim" Fitzsimmons ▪ 1875-1963

U.S. horse trainer who saddled more winners than anyone else in American turf history.

AT AGE 83:

> **"I'll be around as long as the horses think I'm smarter than they are."**

Abraham Flexner ▪ 1866-1959

American educator and teacher.

AT AGE 64:

> **"We must not overlook the important role that extremists play. They are the gadflies that keep society from being too complacent, or self-satisfied; they are, if sound, the spearhead of progress."**

> **"Science, in the very act of solving problems, creates more of them."**

Le Bovier de Fontenelle ▪ 1657-1757

French philosopher and secretary of the French Academy of Sciences for 42 years. His last major work was written when he was 95.

At age 95, replying to a woman of 90 who said to him, "Death has forgotten us":

"Ssssh!"

"Ah, my dear, if only I were 90 again."

At age 99:

"It is high time for me to depart, for at my age I now begin to see things as they really are."

GERALD R. FORD ▪ 1913-

U.S. vice-president who became the thirty-eighth president after Richard Nixon's resignation in 1974.

AT AGE 61:

"Truth is the glue that holds government together."

"I would hope that understanding and reconciliation are not limited to the 19th hole alone."

HENRY FORD ▪ 1863-1947

American industrialist, inventor, and philanthropist. The father of the mass-produced automobile, he was born on a Michigan farm, left school at 16, and died a billionaire.

REGARDING OLD AGE:

> **"Anyone who stops learning is old, whether at 20 or 80. Anyone who keeps learning stays young. The greatest thing in life is to keep your mind young."**

AT AGE 65:

> **"There are two ways of making money—one at the expense of others, the other by service to others."**

> **"The whole secret of a successful life is to find out what it is one's destiny to do, and then do it."**

AT AGE 67:

> **"What we call evil is simply ignorance bumping its head in the dark."**

E. M. FORSTER ▪ 1879-1970

English author, and one of the most important novelists of the 20th century. Best known for *A Passage to India* (1924), he also wrote essays and literary criticism.

AT AGE 7 2:

"Spoon feeding in the long run teaches us nothing but the shape of the spoon."

"Think before you speak is criticism's motto; speak before you think, creation's."

"The only books that influence us are those for which we are ready, and which have gone a little further down our particular path than we have yet gone ourselves."

"America is rather like life. You can usually find in it what you look for."

"Two cheers for Democracy: one be-cause it admits variety and two because it permits criticism."

HARRY E. FOSDICK ▪ 1878-1969

U.S. clergyman. From 1926 until 1946 he preached on the nationwide radio program "National Vespers."

AT AGE 80:

"He who cannot rest, cannot work; he who cannot let go, cannot hold on; he who cannot find footing, cannot go forward."

"Bitterness imprisons life; love releases it. Bitterness paralyzes life; love empow-ers it. Bitterness sours life; love sweet-ens it. Bitterness sickens life; love heals it."

Anatole France ▪ 1844-1924

French novelist, poet, and critic. Probably the most prominent and prolific French man of letters of his time. At age 77 he was awarded the Nobel Prize in Literature.

At age 70:

> **"The average man, who does not know what to do with his life, wants another one which will last forever."**

> **"To die for an idea is to place a pretty high price upon conjectures."**

> **"A tale without love is like beef without mustard, insipid."**

POLLY FRANCIS ▪ 1884-1978

U.S. author, fashion illustrator, and photographer for *Harper's Bazaar* and *Vogue*. Her articles on old age, written when she was in her 90s, were published worldwide.

AT AGE 90:

"What a baffling thing old age is! The area which lies between the 'here' and the 'hereafter' is a difficult passage to travel. One must make the journey to fully understand it."

"Age creeps up so stealthily that it is often with shock that we become aware of its presence. Perhaps that is why so many of us reach old age utterly unprepared to meet its demands."

"The autumn of human life, like the autumn of nature, can bring richness of beauty. A life of the heart and of the mind takes over while our physical force ebbs away."

FELIX FRANKFURTER ▪ 1882-1965

Associate justice of the U.S. Supreme Court. He emigrated to the U.S. from Austria, received his law degree from Harvard, and became a law professor there.

AT AGE 72:

> **"A judge should be compounded of the faculties that are demanded of the historian and the philosopher and the prophet."**

AT AGE 80:

> **"In a democratic society like ours, relief must come through an aroused popular conscience that sears the conscience of the people's representatives."**

Benjamin Franklin ▪ 1706-1790

American statesman, diplomat, inventor, scientist, and printer. He helped draft and signed the Declaration of Independence. He proved that lightning was made up of electricity, invented bifocal spectacles, and published *Poor Richard's Almanack*.

REGARDING AGING:

> **"All would live long but none would be old."**

AT AGE 7 7:

> **"There never was a good war or a bad peace."**

AT AGE 8 1:

> **"Having lived long, I have experienced many instances of being obliged by better information, or fuller consideration, to change opinions even on important subjects which I once thought right but found otherwise."**

AT AGE 83:

> **"Nothing in this world is certain but death and taxes."**

SIGMUND FREUD ▪ 1856-1939

Austrian psychiatrist. As the founder of psychoanalysis he pioneered a new understanding and treatment of mental illness.

AT AGE 74:

> **"The liberty of the individual is no gift of civilization. It was greatest before there was any civilization."**

MILTON FRIEDMAN ▪ 1912-

U.S. economist, best known for his theory that changes in monetary supply precede changes in overall economic activity. He was awarded the Nobel Prize in Economics in 1976.

AT AGE 67:

> **"A society that puts equality ahead of freedom will end up with neither equality nor freedom."**

AT AGE 72:

> **"There is nothing wrong with the United States that a dose of smaller and less-intrusive government will not cure."**

ERICH FROMM ▪ 1900-1980

U.S. psychologist, author, and philosopher. Born in Germany, he practiced psychoanalysis, lectured at Columbia and Yale, and then was on the faculty at Bennington College.

AT AGE 84:

"Both dreams and myths are important communications from ourselves to ourselves."

ROBERT FROST ▪ 1874-1963

American poet who wrote about rural New England. He is the only poet to be awarded four Pulitzer Prizes.

AT AGE 68:

"Happiness makes up in height what it lacks in length."

AT AGE 81:

"I have never started a poem yet whose end I knew. Writing a poem is discovering."

AT AGE 84:

"You've got to love what's lovable, and hate what's hateable. It takes brains to see the difference."

AT AGE 85:

"People are inexterminable—like flies and bedbugs. There will always be some that survive in cracks and crevices."

AT AGE 86:

"Education is the ability to listen to almost anything without losing your temper or self-confidence."

AT AGE 88:

"I cut my own hair. I got sick of barbers because they talk too much. And too much of their talk was about my hair falling out."

J. WILLIAM FULBRIGHT ▪ 1905-1995

American politician, lawyer, and teacher. He was a U.S. senator and founder of the Fulbright Scholarship program.

AT AGE 61:

"Dissent is an act of faith in a democracy. Like medicine, the test of its value is not in its taste, but its effect."

BUCKMINSTER FULLER ▪ 1895-1983

U.S. engineer, architect, author, and developer of the geodesic dome. He was still inventing in his 80s.

AT AGE 69:

> "I just invent, then wait until man comes around to needing what I've invented."

AT AGE 73:

> "Everyone is born a genius, but the process of living de-geniuses them."

AT AGE 74:

> "We are not going to be able to operate our spaceship earth successfully nor much longer unless we see it as a whole spaceship and our fate as common. It has to be everybody or nobody."

AT AGE 80:

> "Dare to be naive."

JOHN KENNETH GALBRAITH ▪ 1908-

American diplomat, economist, and author. An adviser to John F. Kennedy, he also served as U.S. ambassador to India.

AT AGE 61:

> **"There are few ironclad rules of diplomacy, but to one there is no exception. When an official reports that talks were useful, it can safely be concluded that nothing was accomplished."**

AT AGE 69:

> **"Money is a singular thing. It ranks with love as man's greatest source of joy. And with death as his greatest source of anxiety."**

AT AGE 77:

> **"Nothing is so admirable in politics as a short memory."**

"In all life one should comfort the afflicted, but also one should afflict the comfortable, and especially when they are comfortably, contentedly, even happily wrong."

"In any great organization it is far, far safer to be wrong with the majority than to be right alone."

GRETA GARBO ▪ 1905-1990

American film actress born in Sweden. Known as "the Swedish Sphinx," she was an idol of the late-silent and early-talkie eras. Her films included *Anna Christie*, *Anna Karenina*, *Camille*, and *Ninotchka*.

AT AGE 79:

> "The thing I love to see most is an older couple come along the street supporting one another. You don't have to be married, but it means a lot having a partner for life. . . . I don't have one. . . . I regret that."

> "Perhaps I am most pleased at having fought for the right for women to wear trousers."

JOHN NANCE GARNER ▪ 1868-1967

American lawyer who, after 30 years of service in Congress, served as vice-president of the United States (1933-1941). He died two weeks before his 99th birthday.

AT AGE 66:

"Worst damfool mistake I ever made was letting myself be elected vice-president of the United States. I spent eight long years as Mr. Roosevelt's spare tire."

AT AGE 86:

"You have to do a little bragging on yourself even to your relatives. Man doesn't get anywhere without advertising."

JEAN PAUL GETTY ▪ 1892-1976

American business executive who inherited his father's oil business and formed the Getty Oil Co. One of the richest men in the world, he was also a great art collector.

AT AGE 65:

> **"If you can actually count your money, then you are not really a rich man."**

AT AGE 66:

> **"I believe that the able industrial leader who creates wealth and employment is more worthy of historical notice than politicians or soldiers."**

AT AGE 69:

> **"No one can possibly achieve any real and lasting success or 'get rich' in business by being a conformist."**

> **"There are one hundred men seeking security to one able man who is willing to risk his fortune."**

Sir John Gielgud ▪ 1904-

English actor, director, and producer. His portrayal of Hamlet for the Old Vic company, which he repeated more than 500 times, is considered the finest of his generation.

In his mid-70s:

"I am a very timid, cowardly man . . . but once I go out into the theatre, I have great authority and I get great respect and love from all the people working in it—from the stagehands, the costumers, the scene designers and the actors—and this suddenly justifies my entire existence."

At age 80:

"Acting is half shame, half glory. Shame at exhibiting yourself and glory when you can forget yourself."

HERMIONE GINGOLD ▪ 1897-1987

British actress and comedienne. She special-ized in supporting roles—usually character parts portraying aging English ladies with a sharp sense of humor.

AT AGE 74, ABOUT HER ANTIQUE-DEALER BOYFRIEND WHO WAS IN HIS EARLY 30S:

"He loves antiques—I think that's why he fell for me."

AT AGE 89:

"Sometimes I wonder whether I've given up too much for the theatre, but I have one big consolation—money."

"There's nothing so aging as the past—especially when it catches up with you."

William E. Gladstone ▪ 1809-1898

British statesman and orator. He was prime minister four times and leader of the Liberal Party.

AT AGE 69:

> **"The American Constitution is, so far as I can see, the most wonderful work ever struck off at a given time by the brain and purpose of man."**

AT AGE 70:

> **"In Freedom you lay the firmest foundations both of loyalty and order."**

AT AGE 77:

> **"All the world over, I will back the masses against the classes."**

JOHANN VON GOETHE • 1749-1832

German dramatist, poet, lawyer, botanist, politician, physicist, zoologist, and painter. He wrote his first play at 10, and by 16 he had learned Latin, Greek, French, Italian, and English. At 81 he finished his masterpiece, the drama *Faust*, after working on it for half a century.

AT AGE 82:

> **"I am delighted to find that even at my great age ideas come to me, the pursuit and development of which would require another lifetime."**

WILLIAM GOLDING ▪ 1911-1993

English novelist and writer of short stories, essays, and poetry. He was a Nobel Laureate in 1983 at age 73 and is best known for his allegorical cult novel, *Lord of the Flies*. He was knighted when he was 78.

AT AGE 7 2, AFTER WINNING THE NOBEL PRIZE:

> **"My yesterdays walk with me. They keep step, they are faces that peer over my shoulder."**

AT AGE 8 2:

> **"I'd rather there wasn't an afterlife, really. I'd much rather not be me for thousands of years."**

SAMUEL GOLDWYN ▪ 1882-1974

American pioneer movie mogul. He began Goldwyn Pictures, which merged with another studio to become MGM. His films include *Guys & Dolls*, *Wuthering Heights*, and *The Best Years of Our Lives*.

AT AGE 74:

"A wide screen just makes a bad film twice as bad."

AT AGE 80:

"They may retire me, but I am never going to retire."

Ruth Gordon ▪ 1896-1985

American stage and screen actress and playwright. She won an Academy Award at age 72.

AT AGE 74:

> **"Never give up. Get the knack of getting people to help you and also pitch in yourself. A little money helps, but what really gets it right is to never under any conditions face the facts."**

AT AGE 83:

> **"Discussing how old you are is the temple of boredom."**

AT AGE 84:

> **"Courage is very important. Like a muscle, it is strengthened by use."**

Maurice Goudeket ▪ 1889-1977

French writer and third husband of the French novelist Colette.

AT AGE 75:

"I get up before anyone else in my household, not because sleep has deserted me in my advancing years, but because an intense eagerness to live draws me from my bed."

"It is really something of a feat to have lived 75 years, in spite of illnesses, germs, accidents, disasters and wars. And now every fresh day finds me more filled with wonder and better qualified to draw the last drop of delight from it."

"Up until now I have never known time's inexpressible wealth; and my youth had never entirely yielded itself to happiness."

Martha Graham • 1893-1991

American dancer, teacher, and choreographer who established a school of modern dance. She combined the basic movements of the human body and gymnastics with primitive ritual and folk dance.

AT AGE 65, ON HER CHOREOGRAPHY:

> **"You do what you do because you must do it at that instant in time. If it lives, it is because posterity demands it."**

AT AGE 86:

> **"No artist is ahead of his time. He is his time. It is just that the others are behind the times."**

> **"Age is the acceptance of a term of years. But maturity is the glory of years."**

CARY GRANT ▪ 1904-1986

British movie actor noted for his charm and elegance.

AT AGE 75:

> "My formula for living is quite simple. I get up in the morning and I go to bed at night. In between, I occupy myself as best I can."

AT AGE 81:

> "I pretended to be somebody I wanted to be until I finally became that person. Or he became me."

ROBERT GRAVES ▪ 1895-1985

English poet, novelist, essayist, and critic. Generally regarded as the best love poet of his generation, he was professor of poetry at Oxford.

AT AGE 67:

> **"There's no money in poetry, but then there's no poetry in money either."**

> **"The award of a pure gold medal for poetry would flatter the recipient unduly; no poem ever attains such karat purity."**

AT AGE 68:

> **"I don't really feel my poems are mine at all. I didn't create them out of nothing; I owe them to my relations with other people."**

Theodore F. Green ▪ 1867-1966

American politician. He was governor of Rhode Island and then a U.S. Senator until his retirement at the age of 93.

AT AGE 87:

"Most people say that as you get old you have to give up things. I think you get old because you give up things."

Graham Greene ▪ 1904-1991

English novelist and playwright. He was also noted for his short stories, essays, film criticism, and film scripts.

AT AGE 74:

"Our worst enemies are not the ignorant and the simple, however cruel; our worst enemies are the intelligent and corrupt."

Walter Gropius ▪ 1883-1969

German-American architect and educator. A leader in the development of modern functional architecture, he was chairman of the architecture department at Harvard University.

At age 69:

"The architect's task is to bring inert materials to life by relating them to the human being. Thus conceived, his creation is an act of love."

Sir Alec Guinness ▪ 1914-

English stage and screen actor.

At age 72:

"An actor is . . . at his best a kind of unfrocked priest who, for an hour or two, can call on heaven and hell to mesmerize a group of innocents."

EDITH HAMILTON ▪ 1867-1963

American author famous for her historical novels of Greek and Roman life.

AT AGE 65:

> **"A people's literature is the great textbook for real knowledge of them."**

AT AGE 91:

> **"To be able to be caught up into the world of thought—that is to be educated."**

LEARNED HAND ▪ 1872-1961

American jurist who was often called "the 10th Justice of the Supreme Court." After receiving his law degree from Harvard, he spent the next 42 years as a federal court judge.

AT AGE 88:

> **"We shall succeed only so far as we continue that most distasteful of all activity, the intolerable labor of thought."**

W. C. Handy ▪ 1873-1958

American composer and bandleader known as the "Father of the Blues." Despite his blindness, he conducted his own orchestra.

At age 80:

"Life is something like this trumpet. If you don't put anything in it you don't get anything out. And that's the truth."

Thomas Hardy ▪ 1840-1928

English novelist and poet.

At age 78:

"My opinion is that a poet should express the emotion of all the ages and the thought of his own."

Rex Harrison ▪ 1908-1993

English stage and film actor who received many awards for his performances, including his work in *My Fair Lady*.

At age 7O:

> **"Whatever it is that makes a person charming, it needs to remain a mystery; once the charmer is aware of it, it ceases to be a mannerism and becomes an affectation."**

HELEN HAYES ▪ 1900-1993

Grande dame of American film and stage for nearly nine decades. She won two Oscars 40 years apart, the second at the age of 70.

AT AGE 65:

"We rely upon the poets, the philosophers, and the playwrights to articulate what most of us can only feel in joy and sorrow."

AT AGE 73:

"Solitude—walking alone, doing things alone—is the most blessed thing in the world. The mind relaxes and thoughts begin to flow."

AT AGE 88:

"If you rest, you rust."

WILLIAM RANDOLPH HEARST ▪ 1863-1951

American newspaper editor and publisher. The powerful, wealthy, and controversial creator of Hearst Newspapers, he built Hearst Castle for his mistress, Marion Davies.

AT AGE 61:

"The greatest right in the world is the right to be wrong."

KATHARINE HEPBURN ▪ 1909-

American actress who has won three Academy Awards. Best known for her leading roles in fast-paced comedies opposite her longtime good friend Spencer Tracy, she wrote her autobiography after she was 80.

REGARDING OLD AGE:

> **"I have no romantic feelings about age. Either you are interesting at any age or you are not."**

> **"I see more energy, life and spirit in many so-called senior citizens than in numerous young people I've come in contact with."**

AT AGE 66:

> **"Without discipline, there is no life at all."**

> **"Trying to be fascinating is an asinine position to be in."**

HERMANN HESSE ▪ 1877-1962

German-Swiss novelist who was awarded the 1946 Nobel Prize in Literature.

AT AGE 76:

> **"How good and comforting it is that we can forget! Each of us knows what his memory has stored up and can control. None of us, however, can find his way into the chaos of what he has forgotten."**

> **"All old people, whether they know it or not, are in search of the past . . ."**

ALFRED HITCHCOCK ▪ 1899-1980

English-American film director, writer, and producer. A master of suspense, he began his career in the silent-film era.

AT AGE 66:

"Television is like the invention of indoor plumbing. It didn't change people's habits. It just kept them inside the house."

"Seeing a murder on television can . . . help work off one's antagonisms. And if you haven't any antagonisms, the commercials will give you some."

AT AGE 78:

"For me, the cinema is not a slice of life, but a piece of cake."

Thomas Hobbes ▪ 1588-1679

English philosopher who applied the scientific world view to society and had a pessimistic view of human nature.

AT AGE 63:

"The origin of all great and lasting societies consisted not in the good will men had toward each other, but in the mutual fear they had of each other."

"Leisure is the mother of philosophy."

"He that is taken and put into prison or chains is not conquered, though overcome; for he is still an enemy."

"There is no such thing as perpetual tranquillity of mind because life itself is but motion and can never be without desire, nor without fear."

Laura Z. Hobson ▪ 1900-1986

U.S. novelist.

At age 75:

"Why didn't children ever see that they could damage and harm their parents as much as parents could damage and harm children?"

Eric Hoffer ▪ 1902-1983

U.S. author and self-educated social critic and philosopher.

At age 61:

"To dispose a soul to action we must upset its equilibrium."

At age 68:

"Scratch an intellectual and you find a would-be aristocrat who loathes the sight, the sound and the smell of common folk."

> "There would be no society if living to-
> gether depended upon understanding
> each other."

Hans Hofmann ▪ 1880-1966

American painter born in Germany. He was
the leading figure behind the Abstract Expres-
sionist school of painting in the U.S.

At age 68:

> "Whether the artist works directly from
> nature, from memory, or from fantasy,
> nature is always the source of his
> creative impulses."

> "The ability to simplify means to elimi-
> nate the unnecessary so that the neces-
> sary may speak."

OLIVER WENDELL HOLMES ▪
1809-1894

American author, poet, and physician. He was the first dean of Harvard Medical School.

ABOUT OLD AGE:

> **"Youth longs and manhood strives, but age remembers."**

AT AGE 80:

> **"To be 70 years young is sometimes far more cheerful and hopeful than to be 40 years old."**

OLIVER WENDELL HOLMES, JR. ▪ 1841-1935

U.S. Supreme Court justice for 33 years. Son of the poet Oliver Wendell Holmes, he was known as the "Great Dissenter" and a champion of civil liberties.

REGARDING OLD AGE:

"I used to think that the mainspring was broken by 80, although my father kept on writing. I hope I was wrong for I am keeping on in the same way. I like it and want to produce as long as I can."

AT AGE 70:

"Life is a romantic business. It is painting a picture—not doing a sum—but you have to make it a romance, and it will come to the question of how much fire you have in your belly."

ON HIS 90TH BIRTHDAY, WHILE STILL A SUPREME COURT JUDGE:

> **"The riders in a race do not stop short when they reach the goal. There is a little finishing canter before coming to a standstill. . . . The race is over, but the work never is done while the power to work remains. . . . For to live is to function. That is all there is to living."**

AT AGE 92, AFTER SEEING A PRETTY GIRL:

> **"What I wouldn't give to be 70 again."**

HERBERT CLARK HOOVER ▪
1874-1964

Thirty-first U.S. president. He was head of Allied famine-relief operations during World War I and again after World War II.

AT AGE 70:

> "Older men declare war. But it is youth that must fight and die. And it is youth who must inherit the tribulation, the sorrow, and the triumphs that are the aftermath of war."

AT AGE 73:

> "There are only two occasions when Americans respect privacy, especially in presidents. Those are praying and fishing."

BOB HOPE ▪ 1903-

British-American comedian in vaudeville, stage, radio, movies, and TV.

AT AGE 82:

"I have a wonderful makeup crew. They're the people who are restoring the Statue of Liberty."

AT AGE 87:

"I don't generally feel anything until noon, then it's time for my nap."

Edgar Watson Howe ▪ 1853-1937

American editor and author. He was editor and proprietor of the Atchison, Kansas, *Daily Globe*. His autobiography, *Plain People*, was published in 1929.

At age 69:

> "A good scare is worth more to a man than good advice."

At age 73:

> "After a man passes 60, his mischief is mainly in his head."

> "Wit that is kindly is not very witty."

> "The history of mankind is one long record of giving revolution another trial, and limping back at last to sanity, safety, and work."

WILLIAM DEAN HOWELLS ∙
1837-1920

American novelist, editor, and critic. He was a champion of realism in American literature and the literary mentor of Mark Twain.

AT AGE 62:

"In Europe life is histrionic and dramatized, and in America, except when it is trying to be European, it is direct and sincere."

AT AGE 66:

"The mortality of all inanimate things is terrible to me, but that of books most of all."

CHARLES EVANS HUGHES ▪ 1862-1948

American statesman and jurist. He was the governor of New York before President Taft appointed him associate justice of the Supreme Court. In 1930 President Hoover appointed him chief justice.

AT AGE 74:

> **"The history of scholarship is a record of disagreements."**

Victor Hugo • 1802-1885

French poet, novelist, and dramatist. Because he opposed Napoleon III, he was exiled for 18 years, after which he returned to Paris in triumph.

Regarding old age:

> **"Fire is seen in the eyes of the young, but it is light we see in the old man's eyes."**

At age 60:

> **"One is not idle because one is absorbed. There is both visible and invisible labor. To contemplate is to toil. To think is to do."**

> **"There are thoughts which are prayers. There are moments when, whatever the posture of the body, the soul is on its knees."**

At age 80:

> **"Gentlemen, I am 80 and I am beginning my career."**

SOL HUROK ▪ 1888-1974

U.S. impresario. For 65 years, he brought to the U.S. the greatest stars of the performing arts, including A. Segovia, A. Rubinstein, A. Pavlova, R. Nureyev, and the Bolshoi Ballet.

AT AGE 86, REGARDING HOW HE SELECTS PERFORMERS:

"If they're not temperamental, I don't want them. It's the nature of the great artist to be that way."

WILLIAM RALPH INGE ▪ 1860-1954

English prelate and author who was the dean of St. Paul's cathedral (1911-1934).

REGARDING OLD AGE:

> **"Experience is a good teacher, but her fees are very high."**

AT AGE 62:

> **"Literature flourishes best when it is half a trade and half an art."**

AT AGE 63:

> **"A man may build himself a throne of bayonets, but he cannot sit on it."**

AT AGE 72:

> **"The aim of education is the knowledge not of facts but of values."**

Thomas Jefferson ▪ 1743-1826

Third U.S. president and the principal author of the Declaration of Independence. He arranged for the Louisiana Purchase, founded the University of Virginia, and built the mansion at Monticello, his estate.

REGARDING OLD AGE:

> **"The sun has not caught me in bed in fifty years."**

AT AGE 72:

> **"I hope our wisdom will grow with our power and teach us that the less we use our power the greater it will be."**

AT AGE 76:

> **"I was a hard student until I entered on the business of life, the duties of which leave no idle time; and now, retired, at the age of 76, I am again a hard student."**

> **"The boisterous sea of liberty is never without a wave."**

AT AGE 8 2:

> **"When angry, count to 10 before you speak; if very angry, 100."**

LADY BIRD JOHNSON ▪ 1912-

Wife of Lyndon Johnson, the 32d president of the United States. An astute businesswoman, she developed a multimillion-dollar radio and television broadcasting corporation. She acquired her nickname at age 2 when a nursemaid described her as being "as purty as a lady bird."

AT AGE 7 7:

> **"Flowers in a city are like lipstick on a woman—it just makes you look better to have a little color."**

PHILIP JOHNSON ∙ 1906-

American architect, museum curator, and historian. He is best known for functionalist glass and steel buildings in the International Style. His works include the Seagram Building in New York City.

AT AGE 63:

"All architecture is shelter. All great architecture is the design of space that contains, cuddles, exalts, or stimulates the person in that space."

AT AGE 74:

"Architects are pretty much high-class whores. We can turn down projects the way they can turn down some clients, but we've both got to say yes to someone if we want to stay in business."

AT AGE 81:

"All architects want to live beyond their deaths."

MOTHER JONES ▪ 1830-1930

U.S. labor leader. She was an agitator for Appalachian miners and in 1903 led a children's march to the New York home of President Theodore Roosevelt to dramatize the evils of child labor.

AT AGE 90, WHEN A JUDGE ASKED WHO HAD ISSUED HER A PERMIT TO SPEAK ON THE STREETS:

"Patrick Henry, Thomas Jefferson, and John Adams."

AT AGE 95:

"Pray for the dead and fight like hell for the living."

CARL GUSTAV JUNG ∎ 1875-1961

Swiss psychiatrist who made monumental contributions to the field of analytical psychology.

REGARDING OLD AGE:

"A human being would certainly not grow to be 70 or 80 years old if this longevity had no meaning for the species to which he belongs."

AT AGE 67:

"No one can flatter himself that he is immune to the spirit of his own epoch, or even that he possesses a full understanding of it."

AT AGE 68:

"Where love rules, there is no will to power; and where power predominates, there love is lacking."

> "If one does not understand a person, one tends to regard him as a fool."

AT AGE 81:

> "The unexpected and the incredible belong in this world. Only then is life whole."

GARSON KANIN ▪ 1912-

American playwright, director, author, and screenwriter. He directed the plays *The Diary of Anne Frank* and *Funny Girl*.

AT AGE 65:

"Your outlook, your frame of mind, as you advance in years is what matters most."

"Life is not, or should not be, a spectator sport. It must be lived, not just observed."

"Maturing men and women must avoid ruts, fixed habits, old ways. The antidote to aging is action, both physical and mental, and learning."

Canadian photographer and journalist.

AT AGE 70:

"I have found that great people have in common an immense belief in themselves and in their mission. They also have great determination and an ability to work hard. At the crucial moment of decision, they draw on their accumulated wisdom. Above all, they have integrity."

Helen Keller ▪ 1880-1968

American educator and author who was blind and deaf from the age of two. Under the devoted teaching of Anne Sullivan, she learned to speak eloquently and to communicate by means of a manual alphabet pressed into her hand. She graduated with honors from Radcliffe and was an inspiration to millions.

AT AGE 60:

"To keep our faces toward change and behave like free spirits in the presence of fate is strength undefeatable."

AT AGE 75, TO A BLIND 5-YEAR-OLD CHILD:

"Never bend your head. Always hold it high. Look the world straight in the face."

AT AGE 77:

"Security is mostly superstition. . . . Avoiding danger is no safer in the long run than outright exposure. Life is either a daring adventure, or nothing."

CHARLES FRANKLIN KETTERING ▪ 1876-1958

U.S. engineer and inventor.

AT AGE 73:

"We should all be concerned about the future because we will have to spend the rest of our lives there."

JIDDU KRISHNAMURTI ▪ 1895-1986

Indian mystic with an active career in lecturing and writing. He finally settled in Ojai, California, where, starting in 1969, he headed the Krishnamurti Foundation.

AT AGE 67:

"I maintain that Truth is a pathless land, and you cannot approach it by any path whatsoever, by any religion, by any sect."

MAGGIE KUHN ▪ 1905-

U.S. social worker and civil rights activist. She was an organizer of the Gray Panthers (1970), a group dedicated to improving conditions for senior citizens.

AT AGE 67:

> **"Arbitrary retirement at a fixed age ought to be negotiated and decided according to the wishes of the people involved. Mandatory retirement ought to be illegal."**

AT AGE 70:

> **"Power should not be concentrated in the hands of so few, and powerlessness in the hands of so many."**

AT AGE 74:

"Old age is not a disease—it is strength and survivorship, triumph over all kinds of vicissitudes and disappointments, trials and illnesses."

"I think of age as a great universalizing force. It's the only thing we all have in common. Life is a continuum. Only we, in our stupidity and blindness, have chopped it up into little pieces and kept all those little pieces separate."

"Our technological society scrap-piles old people as it does automobiles."

AT AGE 86:

"I'm having a glorious old age. One of my greatest delights is that I have outlived most of my opposition."

STANLEY KUNITZ ▪ 1905-

American Pulitzer Prize-winning poet, professor, and consultant to the Library of Congress.

AT AGE 79:

"Old myths, old gods, old heroes have never died. They are only sleeping at the bottom of our mind, waiting for our call. We have need for them. They represent the wisdom of our race."

DOROTHEA LANGE ▪ 1895-1979

American photographer. She portrayed workers' essential dignity and pride, and documented rural America for the federal government and *Life* magazine.

AT AGE 83:

"The camera is an instrument that teaches people how to see without a camera."

Suzanne K. Langer ▪ 1895-1985

A leading American philosopher. She exerted a profound influence on the fields of psychology, philosophy, and the social sciences.

AT AGE 62:

> **"If we would have new knowledge, we must get a whole world of new questions."**

AT AGE 72:

> **"Art is the objectivity of feeling."**

Eva Le Gallienne ▪ 1899-1991

English-American actress, producer, director, teacher, and author. She founded and ran the New York Civic Repertory Theatre. In her late 70s she toured in a revival of *The Royal Family*.

At age 66:

> **"No mechanical device can ever take the place of that mysterious communication between players and the public, that sense of an experience directly shared which gives to the living theatre its unique appeal."**

> **"Innovators are inevitably controversial."**

Ninon de Lenclos • 1620-1705

French beauty and wit. She gathered in her Paris salon notables who paid well for her sexual favors. She was also admired for her sound business sense.

REGARDING OLD AGE:

"If God had to give a woman wrinkles, he might at least have put them on the soles of her feet."

JOHN L. LEWIS ▪ 1880-1969

American labor leader. He had an important role in the American Federation of Labor (AFL) until he split with it (1935) and founded the Committee for Industrial Organization (CIO). He resigned as president of the United Mine Workers of America at the age of 80.

AT AGE 65:

"Everything of importance in this world has been accomplished by the free inquiring spirit. The preservation of that spirit is more important than any social system."

ANNE MORROW LINDBERGH ▪ 1907-

American writer and poet. The wife of Charles Lindbergh, she had to endure the 1932 kidnap and murder of her first son. At 82 years of age she wrote *The Prisoner of Pineapple Place*, but *Gift from the Sea* (1955) remains her most famous book.

AT AGE 66:

"It isn't for the moment you are struck that you need courage, but for the long uphill climb back to sanity and faith and security."

AT AGE 67:

"Love is a force. It is not a result; it is a cause. It is not a product; it is power, like money, or steam, or electricity."

Walter Lippmann ▪ 1889-1974

American essayist and editor. The writer of a highly influential syndicated column for the New York *Herald Tribune* and the Washington *Post*, he was awarded a special Pulitzer Prize citation for news analysis and for international reporting.

AT AGE 66:

"When distant and unfamiliar and complex things are communicated to great masses of people, the truth suffers a considerable and often a radical distortion."

AT AGE 72:

"I don't think old men ought to promote wars for young men to fight. I don't like warlike old men."

AT AGE 74:

"Industry is a better horse to ride than genius."

"Men who are orthodox when they are young are in danger of being middle-aged all their lives."

ANITA LOOS ▪ 1893-1981

American writer of plays and movie scripts.

AT AGE 81:

"France is the thriftiest of all nations. To a Frenchman sex provides the most economical way to have fun. The French are a logical race."

"Pleasure that isn't paid for is as insipid as everything else that's free."

"Those women's liberationists keep getting up on soapboxes and proclaiming women are brighter than men. That's true, but it should be kept quiet or it ruins the whole racket."

CLARE BOOTH LUCE ▪ 1903-1989

American editor, playwright, and diplomat. The wife of Henry Luce, she was managing editor of *Vogue* and *Vanity Fair*, a member of Congress, and ambassador to Italy.

AT AGE 76:

"Courage is the ladder on which all other virtues mount."

AT AGE 78:

"I don't have a warm personal enemy left. They've all died off. I miss them terribly because they helped define me."

Douglas MacArthur ▪ 1880-1964

Army officer in World War I who became the most decorated military man in U.S. history. Although he retired in 1937, he was recalled in World War II to be supreme Allied commander in the southwest Pacific. He liberated the Philippines and accepted the Japanese surrender in 1945.

At age 65:

> **"Nobody grows old by merely living a number of years. People grow old only by deserting their ideals."**

At age 75:

> **"There is no security on this earth; there is only opportunity."**

> **"Can war be outlawed? If so, it would mark the greatest advance in civilization since the Sermon on the Mount."**

SIR COMPTON MACKENZIE ▪
1883-1972

English author particularly noted for his novels set in exotic locations.

AT AGE 87:

> **"I find now at 87 that I forget people's names occasionally and more regrettably, owing to my wretched eyesight, people's faces, but mercifully my power to concentrate on work has not in the least diminished."**

ARCHIBALD MacLEISH ▪ 1892-1982

American poet, playwright, editor, lawyer, professor, and farmer. He was librarian of Congress and undersecretary of state during the administration of Franklin D. Roosevelt. His *Collected Poems 1917-1952* earned him a Pulitzer Prize.

AT AGE 64:

"The dissenter is every human being at those moments of his life when he resigns momentarily from the herd and thinks for himself."

AT AGE 67:

"Journalism is concerned with events, poetry with feelings. Journalism is concerned with the look of the world, poetry with the feel of the world."

"The business of the law is to make sense of the confusion of what we call human life—to reduce it to order but at the same time to give it possibility, scope, even dignity."

"Poets are literal-minded men who will squeeze a word till it hurts."

Harold MacMillan ▪ 1894-1986

English statesman active in World War II. He took over the post of prime minister (1957-63) after the Suez Canal crisis shook up the British government.

At age 64:

"At home you always have to be a politician. When you are abroad you almost feel yourself a statesman."

"Tradition does not mean that the living are dead, it means the dead are living."

At age 67:

"As usual the Liberals offer a mixture of sound and original ideas. Unfortunately none of the sound ideas is original and none of the original ideas is sound."

At age 69:

"A man who trusts nobody is apt to be the kind of man nobody trusts."

GOLO MANN ▪ 1909-

German historian, and son of Thomas Mann.

AT AGE 78:

"Man is always more than he can know of himself. Consequently, his accomplishments, time and again, will come as a surprise to him."

THOMAS MANN ▪ 1875-1955

German novelist and essayist known for his forceful, eloquent style. He was awarded the Nobel Prize in Literature (1929).

AT AGE 64:

"Hold fast the time! Guard it, watch over it, every hour, every minute! Unregarded it slips away like a lizard, smooth, slippery. . . . Hold every moment sacred."

Marya Mannes ▪ 1904-1990

American author, journalist, and critic of radio, television, and theater. She was an early supporter of women's rights.

At age 60:

"Nobody objects to a woman being a good writer or sculptor or geneticist as long as she manages also to be a good wife, mother, good-looking, good-tempered, well-dressed, well-groomed, and unaggressive."

"In an age where the lowered eyelid is merely a sign of fatigue, the delicate game of love is pining away."

"For every five well-adjusted and smoothly functioning Americans, there are two who never had the chance to discover themselves. It may well be because they have never been alone with themselves."

MAO ZEDONG ▪ 1893-1976

Chairman of the Chinese Communist Party and of the People's Republic of China. It is said that his book, *Quotations from the Works of Mao Zedong,* was the second most popular publication in history.

AT AGE 65:

"A revolution does not march a straight line. It wanders where it can, retreats before superior forces, advances wherever it has room, attacks whenever the enemy retreats or bluffs, and, above all, is possessed of enormous patience."

"I have witnessed the tremendous energy of the masses. On this foundation it is possible to accomplish any task whatsoever."

Thurgood Marshall ▪ 1908-1993

U.S. jurist and lawyer. He headed the legal staff of the National Association for the Advancement of Colored People (NAACP), and then became the first black to serve as associate justice of the Supreme Court. He retired at the age of 83.

AT AGE 61:

"Our whole constitutional heritage rebels at the thought of giving government the power to control men's minds."

"If the First Amendment means anything, it means that a state has no business telling a man, sitting alone in his own house, what books he may read or what films he may watch."

Groucho Marx ▪ 1890-1977

American movie and television comedian. A member of the Marx Brothers team, he starred on *You Bet Your Life*, television's first comedy show with a quiz-show format.

Regarding old age:

"A man is only as old as the woman he feels."

"Growing old is something you do if you're lucky."

At age 64:

"There's only one way to find out if a man is honest: Ask him. If he says yes, you know he's a crook."

"Years ago I tried to top everybody, but I don't anymore. I realized it was killing conversation. When you're always trying for a topper you aren't really listening. It ruins communication."

"Some people claim that marriage interferes with romance. There's no doubt about it. Anytime you have a romance, your wife is bound to interfere."

John Masefield ▪ 1878–1967

Poet Laureate of England for 37 years, until his death at age 89. He also wrote plays, novels, and adventure stories for children.

At age 80:

> "In the power and splendor of the universe, inspiration waits for the millions to come. Man has only to strive for it. Poems greater than the *Iliad*, plays greater than *Macbeth*, stories more engaging than *Don Quixote* await their seeker and finder."

At age 85:

> "There are few earthly things more beautiful than a university . . . a place where those who hate ignorance may strive to know, where those who perceive truth may strive to make others see it."

Henri Matisse ▪ 1869-1954

French artist best known for his still lifes. In his later years he specialized in stencils and paper cutouts (decoupage). He was also an accomplished sculptor and lithographer.

AT AGE 81:

"You study, you learn, but you guard the original naiveté. It has to be within you as love is within the lover."

W. SOMERSET MAUGHAM ▪
1874-1965

Prolific English writer of short stories, plays, and novels. One of the world's most successful authors, he claimed to have sold more than 64 million copies of his books, which would make him the most widely read British writer since Charles Dickens.

AT AGE 64:

"Old age has its pleasures, which, though different, are not less than the pleasures of youth."

"There is no explanation for evil. It must be looked upon as a necessary part of the order of the universe. To ignore it is childish, to bewail it is senseless."

AT AGE 67:

> "If a nation values anything more than freedom, it will lose its freedom; and the irony of it is that if it is comfort or money that it values more, it will lose that, too."

IN HIS MID-80S:

> "Old age is ready to undertake tasks that youth shirked because they would take too long."

AT AGE 91, TO HIS NEPHEW:

> "You know that I'm at death's door. But the trouble is that I'm afraid to knock."

André Maurois • 1885-1967

French biographer, novelist, and essayist.

At age 70:

"A successful marriage is an edifice that must be rebuilt every day."

"The really great novel . . . tends to be the exact negative of its author's life."

At age 78:

"In literature as in love, we are astonished at what is chosen by others."

Elsa Maxwell • 1883-1963

American hostess who considered herself the most famous party giver in the world.

At age 75:

"Laugh at yourself first, before anyone else can."

Barbara McClintock ▪ 1902–

American scientist who received the Nobel Prize in Medicine (1983) for genetic research.

At age 81:

"If you know you are on the right track, if you have this inner knowledge, then nobody can turn you off . . . regardless of what they say."

Alexander Meiklejohn ▪ 1872–1964

American educator. He taught philosophy and logic at Brown and Cornell.

At age 83:

"Suppression is always foolish. Freedom is always wise."

GOLDA MEIR ▪ 1898-1978

Israeli stateswoman. Born in the U.S., she became at age 71 the first woman premier of Israel.

AT AGE 75:

"Old age is like a plane flying through a storm. Once you are aboard there is nothing you can do."

"At work, you think of the children you have left at home. At home, you think of the work you have left unfinished. Such a struggle is unleashed within yourself, your heart is rent."

Dr. Karl Menninger ▪ 1893-1990

American psychiatrist, author, and professor.

AT AGE 65:

"Unrest of spirit is a mark of life."

AT AGE 66:

"Money giving is a very good criterion of a person's mental health. Generous people are rarely mentally ill people."

ROBERT MENZIES ▪ 1894-1978

Australian Liberal politician and prime minister.

AT AGE 76:

> **"Men of genius are not to be analyzed by commonplace rules. The rest of us will do well to remember two things. One is never to forget posterity when devising a policy. The other is never to think of posterity when making a speech."**

MICHELANGELO ▪ 1475-1564

Sculptor, painter, architect, and poet of the Italian Renaissance whose most famous works include the *Pietà* and *David* sculptures and the ceiling of the Sistine Chapel. At 71 he was appointed chief architect of St. Peter's in Rome, which he continued working on until his death at age 89.

AT AGE 79:

> **"The marble not yet carved can hold the form of every thought the greatest artist has."**

JAMES MICHENER ▪ 1907-

U.S. novelist noted for best-selling books about exotic places. His *Tales of the South Pacific* was awarded the 1948 Pulitzer Prize in Fiction.

AT AGE 78:

> **"The really great writers are people like Emily Brontë who sit in a room and write out of their limited experience and unlimited imagination."**

AT AGE 82:

> **"I was brought up in the great tradition of the late 19th century: that a writer never complains, never explains, and never disdains."**

HENRY MILLER ▪ 1891-1980

American author whose sexually candid novels were banned in the U.S. and Great Britain until the 1960s.

REGARDING OLD AGE:

"Youth has to do with spirit, not age. Men of 70 and 80 are often more youthful than the young. Theirs is the real youth."

AT AGE 60:

"Until it is kindled by a spirit as flamingly alive as the one which gave it birth, a book is dead to us. Words divested of their magic are but dead hieroglyphs."

AT AGE 66:

"One's destination is never a place but rather a new way of looking at things."

AT AGE 80:

> **"A short life and a merry one is far better than a long life sustained by fear, caution, and perpetual medical surveillance."**

AT AGE 81:

> **"I really thought I could do something to change the world. I soon found out you can't change the world. The best you can do is learn to live with it."**

French dancer and singer.

AT AGE 82:

"A kiss can be a comma, a question mark, or an exclamation point. That's basic spelling that every woman ought to know."

Claude Monet ■ 1840-1926

Father of French Impressionist painting and one of the foremost landscape painters in the history of art. At age 73 he began working on his last series of water lilies, 19 huge canvases painted in his own garden. Despite failing eyesight he painted until shortly before his death at 86.

AT AGE 67:

"You must know I'm totally absorbed in my work. These landscapes of water and reflections have become an obsession. It's quite beyond my powers at my age, and yet I want to succeed in expressing what I feel."

AT AGE 80:

"My work belongs to the public, and people can say what they like about it; I've done what I could."

Italian educator, pioneer of preschool education, and Italy's first female doctor. She originated the Montessori method of education.

At age 79:

> **"If education is always to be conceived along the same antiquated lines of a mere transmission of knowledge, there is little to be hoped from it in the bettering of man's future. For what is the use of transmitting knowledge if the individual's total development lags behind?"**

> **"The only language men ever speak perfectly is the one they learn in babyhood, when no one can teach them anything!"**

PIERRE MONTEUX ▪ 1875–1964

French orchestra conductor.

ON HIS 89TH BIRTHDAY:

"I still have two abiding passions. One is my model railway, the other—women. But, at the age of 89, I find I am getting just a little too old for model railways."

GEORGE MOORE ▪ 1852–1933

Irish-born author who lived in Paris. He introduced naturalism to the Victorian novel.

AT AGE 64:

"A man travels the world in search of what he needs and returns home to find it."

HENRY MOORE ▪ 1898-1986

British sculptor who fused elements of modern abstract art with primitive and traditional concepts in his treatment of the human figure.

AT AGE 69:

> "A sculptor is a person obsessed with the form and shape of things, and it's not just the shape of one thing, but the shape of anything and everything: the growth of a flower; the hard tense strength although delicate form of a bone; the strong solid fleshiness of a beech tree trunk."

Samuel Eliot Morison · 1887-1976

U.S. historian, Harvard University professor, and official U.S. naval historian for World War II. He was awarded two Pulitzer Prizes in Biography (1943 and 1958).

AT AGE 78:

> **"If the American Revolution had produced nothing but the Declaration of Independence, it would have been worthwhile."**

John, Lord Morley · 1838-1923

English statesman, editor of *Fortnightly Review*, and one of the best biographers of his time. A member of Parliament, he was also a supporter of William Gladstone, and chief secretary for Ireland.

AT AGE 70:

> **"No man can climb out beyond the limitations of his own character."**

American painter. She began to paint at age 76, when arthritis made her give up embroidery. Her pictures were "discovered" when she was 78, after which she had more than 200 exhibitions. She was still painting at age 100.

AT AGE 93, WHEN ASKED OF WHAT SHE WAS PROUDEST IN HER LIFE:

> **"I've helped some people."**

AT AGE 100:

> **"Paintin's not important. The important thing is keepin' busy."**

> **"Much as I enjoy visiting with my friends and neighbors, I have come to see that *one* 100-year celebration is enough for anybody, and I would like to spend my 101st birthday the same as my first day—very quiet."**

English journalist who served with the Intelligence Corps in World War II. He received the Legion of Honor award and the Croix de Guerre. In later years he was editor of *Punch* and a television reporter/interviewer.

AT AGE 60:

> **"This horror of pain is a rather low instinct and . . . if I think of human beings I've known and of my own life, I can't recall any case of pain which didn't, on the whole, enrich life."**

AT AGE 63:

> **"Old politicians, like old actors, revive in the limelight."**

AT AGE 65:

> **"Bad humor is an evasion of reality; good humor is an acceptance of it."**

Dr. Margaret Murray • 1863-1963

British archeologist and the first woman Egyptologist. She published more than 80 books on ancient Egypt.

At age 100:

> "At my age I stand . . . on a high peak alone. I have no contemporaries with whom I can exchange memories or views. But that very isolation gives me a less biased view of that vast panorama of human life which is spread before the eyes of a centenarian, still more when those eyes are the eyes of an archeologist. It is true that much of the far distance is shrouded in cloud and mist, but every here and there the fog thins a little and one can see clearly the advance of mankind."

LOUISE NEVELSON ▪ 1899-1988

American sculptor who constructed huge walls or enclosed box arrangements of complex and rhythmic abstract shapes. She used odd pieces of wood, found objects, cast metal, and other materials.

AT AGE 73:

> **"If I have sorrow or enjoyment, my works go along with me. Somehow they have a life of their own and they reflect me."**

AT AGE 75:

> **"The freer that women become, the freer men will be. Because when you enslave someone—you are enslaved."**

AT AGE 77:

> **"What we call reality is an agreement that people have arrived at to make life more livable."**

AT AGE 81:

> **"I never feel age. . . . If you have creative work, you don't have age or time."**

Cardinal John Henry Newman ▪ 1801-1890

English churchman, cardinal of the Roman Catholic Church, a founder of the Oxford Movement, and master of English prose.

AT AGE 67:

"Living Nature, not dull Art, shall plan my ways and rule my heart."

AT AGE 72:

"It is almost the definition of a gentleman to say that he is one who never inflicts pain."

Pat Nixon ▪ 1912-1993

Wife of U.S. President Richard M. Nixon.

AT AGE 60:

"Being First Lady is the hardest unpaid job in the world."

RICHARD MILHOUS NIXON ∎
1913-1994

Thirty-seventh president of the United States, and a lawyer. He reopened relations with the People's Republic of China in 1972. Because of his implication in the Watergate scandal, he was the first president to resign from office (1974).

AT AGE 61:

> **"Always remember, others may hate you. Those who hate you don't win unless you hate them. And then you destroy yourself."**

AT AGE 67:

> **"Life isn't meant to be easy. It's hard to take being on the top—or on the bottom. . . . Life is one crisis after another."**

AT AGE 77:

> **"I played by the rules of politics as I found them."**

SEAN O'CASEY ▪ 1881-1964

Irish dramatist. His realistic, often humorous, and ultimately tragic dramas treat aspects of the Irish movement for independence.

AT AGE 75:

> **"Laughter is wine for the soul—laughter soft, or loud and deep, tinged through with seriousness . . . the hilarious declaration made by man that life is worth living."**

> **"The hallway of every man's life is paved with pictures; all useful, for if we are wise, we can learn from them a richer and braver way to live."**

AT AGE 81:

> **"When one has reached 81, one likes to sit back and let the world turn by itself, without trying to push it."**

Georgia O'Keeffe ▪ 1887-1986

One of the greatest American artists of the 20th century, whose paintings of flowers and desert scenes were highly symbolic. The more than 500 photographs husband Alfred Stieglitz took of her have been called "the greatest love poem in the history of photography."

At age 88:

"The meaning of a word—to me—is not as exact as the meaning of a color."

At age 89:

"Where I was born and how I have lived is unimportant. It is what I have done with where I have been that should be of interest."

At age 89, regarding her painting:

"I had to create an equivalent for what I felt about what I was looking at—not copy it."

Sir Laurence Olivier ▪ 1907-1989

English stage and film star, and film director. Known for his large repertoire and particularly his Shakespearean heroes, he is often cited as the best modern actor.

AT AGE 63:

"I don't know what is better than the work that is given to the actor—to teach the human heart the knowledge of itself."

AT AGE 79:

"Surely we have always acted; it is an instinct inherent in all of us. Some of us are better at it than others, but we all do it."

LINUS PAULING ▪ 1901-1994

U.S. chemist who advocated large doses of vitamin C to prevent the common cold. A staunch supporter of nuclear disarmament, he was awarded the 1954 Nobel Prize in Chemistry and the 1962 Nobel Peace Prize.

AT AGE 62, ACCEPTING HIS SECOND NOBEL PRIZE:

> **"I am confident that we shall in the course of time be enabled to build a world characterized by economic, political, and social justice for all human beings."**

Ivan Petrovich Pavlov ▪ 1849-1936

Russian physiologist and experimental psychologist who studied the nature and development of conditioned reflexes in the early 1890s. He was awarded the Nobel Prize in Physiology or Medicine in 1904.

AT AGE 87:

"Facts are the air of scientists. Without them you never can fly."

"Gradualness, gradualness, and gradualness. From the very beginning of your work, school yourself to severe gradualness in the accumulation of knowledge."

Norman Vincent Peale ▪ 1898-1993

American clergyman, prominent religious author, and radio preacher on the national program "The Art of Living." His final book, *This Incredible Century*, was published in 41 languages.

AT AGE 63:

> **"There is a real magic in enthusiasm. It spells the difference between mediocrity and accomplishment. . . . It gives warmth and good feeling to all your personal relationships."**

AT AGE 87:

> **"We are capable of greater things than we realize."**

CLAUDE PEPPER ▪ 1900-1989

U.S. senator and representative, and champion for America's senior citizens. He fought for such programs as Social Security, minimum wage, and medical assistance for the elderly and for handicapped children.

REGARDING OLD AGE:

"I am told more than 125,000 people in the U.S. have reached the age of 100. Let us hope that everybody can someday look forward to that wonderful privilege."

PABLO PICASSO ▪ 1881-1973

Spanish painter, sculptor, graphic artist, and ceramicist. Generally considered the foremost figure in 20th-century art, he created more than 20,000 works.

REGARDING OLD AGE:

"We don't grow older, we grow riper."

"Age only matters when one is aging. Now that I have arrived at a great age, I might just as well be 20."

AT AGE 68:

"We artists are indestructible; even in prison, or in a concentration camp, I would be almighty in my own world of art, even if I had to paint my pictures with my wet tongue on the dusty floor of my cell."

At age 77:

> "Art is the lie that enables us to realize the truth."

At age 83:

> "Painting . . . is a form of magic designed as a mediator between this strange hostile world and us, a way of seizing the power by giving form to our terrors as well as our desires."

At age 84:

> "I am only a public entertainer who has understood his time."

MARY PICKFORD ▪ 1890-1979

American leading lady of the silent screen. She established United Artists Corporation with her husband Douglas Fairbanks, Charlie Chaplin, and D. W. Griffith.

REGARDING OLD AGE:

> **"When I was just a child, I was forced to live far beyond my years; now I have reversed the order and I intend to remain young indefinitely."**

Max Planck ▪ 1858-1947

German physicist who began modern physics with his proposal of the quantum theory. He was awarded the Nobel Prize in Physics in 1918.

AT AGE 78:

"An important scientific innovation rarely makes its way by gradually winning over and converting its opponents. . . . Its opponents gradually die out and the growing generation is familiar with the idea from the beginning."

PLATO ▪ 427-347 B.C.

Greek philosopher, and student of Socrates.

REGARDING THE PROCESS OF AGING:

"The spiritual eyesight improves as the physical eyesight declines."

REGARDING OLD AGE:

"He who is of a calm and happy nature will hardly feel the pressure of age, but to him who is of an opposite disposition, youth and age are equally a burden."

"It gives me great pleasure to converse with the aged. They have been over the road that all of us must travel and know where it is rough and where it is level and easy."

George Washington Plunkett ▪ 1842–1924

American politician.

AT AGE 63:

"The politician who steals is worse than a fool. With all the grand opportunities around for the man with political pull, there's no excuse for stealin' a cent."

Sir Karl Popper ▪ 1902–

Austrian-born English philosopher.

AT AGE 61:

"Our belief in any particular natural law cannot have a safer basis than our unsuccessful critical attempts to refute it."

AT AGE 80:

"Science may be described as the art of systematic oversimplification."

KATHERINE ANNE PORTER ▪
1890-1980

One of America's most distinguished writers. Many of her short stories are based on the facts of her early life in the South.

AT AGE 73:

> **"Human life itself may be almost pure chaos, but the work of the artist is to take these handfuls of confusion and disparate things and put them together in a frame to give them some kind of shape and meaning."**

> **"There are so many things we are capable of, that we could be or do. The potentialities are so great that we never, any of us, are more than one-fourth fulfilled."**

> **"You do not create a style. You work, and develop yourself; your style is an emanation from your own being."**

AT AGE 80:

"I'm not afraid of life and I'm not afraid of death. Dying's the bore."

ANTHONY POWELL ▪ 1905-

English author, known for social satire.

AT AGE 68:

"Growing old is like being increasingly penalized for a crime you haven't committed."

AT AGE 81:

"The whole idea of interviews is in itself absurd. One cannot answer deep questions about what one's life was like; one writes novels about it."

J. B. PRIESTLEY ▪ 1894-1984

English novelist, dramatist, and essayist. He was noted for ingenious works in which he distorted the normal sequence of past, present, and future, thereby evoking the phenomenon of déjà vu.

REGARDING OLD AGE:

> **"When I was young there was no respect for the young, and now that I am old there is no respect for the old. I missed out coming and going."**

AT AGE 63, REGARDING TELEVISION:

> **"Already we viewers, when not viewing, have begun to whisper to one another that the more we elaborate our means of communication, the less we communicate."**

AT AGE 75:

> **"There can be a rewarding relationship between the sevens and the seventy-fives. They are both closer to the world of mythology and magic than all the busier people between those ages."**

V. S. Pritchett ▪ 1900-

British author and critic.

At age 67:

"I come from a set of storytellers and moralists. . . . The storytellers were forever changing the tale, and the moralists tampering with it in order to put it in an edifying light."

At age 71:

"Youth is the period of assumed personalities and disguises. It is the time of the sincerely insincere."

At age 86:

"It is less the business of the novelist to tell us what happened than to show how it happened."

JEANETTE RANKIN • 1880-1973

U.S. politician and social worker. She was the first U.S. congresswoman, serving from 1917 to 1919 and 1941 to 1943, and an active suffragist and pacifist.

AT AGE 86, CALLING FOR MORE WOMEN IN PUBLIC OFFICE:

"We're half the people; we should be half the Congress."

RONALD REAGAN • 1911-

Fortieth president of the U.S. A former sportscaster, movie actor, rancher, businessman, and author, he championed right-wing causes after joining the Republican Party in 1962.

AT AGE 67:

"Politics is supposed to be the second-oldest profession. I have come to realize that it bears a very close resemblance to the first."

AT AGE 69:

"I was alarmed by my doctor's report; he said I was sound as a dollar."

AFTER AGE 69:

"Since I came to the White House I got two hearing aids, a colon operation, skin cancer, a prostate operation, and I was shot. The damn thing is, I've never felt better in my life."

AT AGE 70:

"*Status quo*—you know—is Latin for 'the mess we're in.' "

AT AGE 71:

"Democracy is not a fragile flower; still, it needs cultivating."

THEODOR REIK ▪ 1888-1969

American psychologist and author. Born in Vienna, he was one of Freud's earliest and most brilliant students.

AT AGE 70:

> **"In our civilization, men are afraid they will not be men enough and women are afraid that they may be considered only women."**

Agnes Repplier ▪ 1858-1950

American author and social critic esteemed for her scholarship and wit.

At age 78:

> **"People who cannot recognize a palpable absurdity are very much in the way of civilization."**

> **"Humor brings insight and tolerance. Irony brings a deeper and less friendly understanding."**

JAMES RESTON ▪ 1909-

American author and journalist. A Washington correspondent and columnist for *The New York Times*, he twice won the Pulitzer Prize: for National Correspondence (1945) and for National Reporting (1957).

AT AGE 75:

"An election is a bet on the future, not a popularity test of the past."

AT AGE 82:

"In foreign policy you have to wait 25 years to see how it comes out."

Jean Rhys ▪ 1894-1979

British novelist born in the Dominican Republic whose works were rediscovered by feminists in the 1970s.

AT AGE 85:

> **"Age seldom arrives smoothly or quickly. It's more often a succession of jerks."**

George Hyman Rickover ▪ 1900-1986

American naval officer. Known as "Father of the Nuclear Navy," he directed the development of nuclear-powered submarines and retired unwillingly after 63 years of active duty.

AT AGE 79:

> **"If you're going to sin, sin against God, not the bureaucracy; God will forgive you but the bureaucracy won't."**

AT AGE 81:

> **"The more you sweat in peace, the less you bleed in war."**

John D. Rockefeller ▪ 1839-1937

U.S. financier, philanthropist, and oil magnate. He founded Standard Oil of Ohio, which was consolidated to form Standard Oil Trust and then deemed illegal and dissolved.

AT AGE 60 HE MADE THESE RULES, AND HE FOLLOWED THEM THE REST OF HIS LIFE:

1. **Never lose interest in life and the world.**
2. **Eat sparingly and at regular hours.**
3. **Take plenty of exercise but not too much.**
4. **Get plenty of sleep.**
5. **Never allow yourself to become annoyed.**
6. **Set a daily schedule of life and keep it.**
7. **Get a lot of sunlight.**
8. **Drink as much milk as will agree with you.**
9. **Obey your doctor and consult him often.**
10. **Don't overdo things.**

AT AGE 85:

> **"My supreme thought on my 85th birthday is one of inexpressible gratitude for the opportunities which life has brought me of being of service to my fellow men."**

JOHN D. ROCKEFELLER, JR. ▪ 1874-1960

American philanthropist. Son of John D. Rockefeller, he devoted his life to charitable use of his family fortune. He gave major financial support to Rockefeller Center, Radio City, the Cloisters, and Lincoln Center in New York City; and to the restoration of Colonial Williamsburg, Virginia.

AT AGE 82, REGARDING WEALTH:

> **"I was born into it [wealth] and there was nothing I could do about it. It was there, like air or food or any other element. . . . The only question with wealth is what you do with it."**

Norman Rockwell ▪ 1894-1978

U.S. illustrator and painter who specialized in warm and humorous scenes of everyday small-town American life. His style of finely drawn realism was featured on covers of the *Saturday Evening Post*.

AT AGE 78:

> **"I unconsciously decided that even if it wasn't an ideal world, it should be, and so I painted only the ideal aspects of it."**

Ginger Rogers ▪ 1911-

Actress and America's dancing sweetheart. In many classic movie musicals she shared the spotlight with Fred Astaire.

AT AGE 76:

> **"When two people love each other, they don't look at each other. They look in the same direction."**

HELENA RUBENSTEIN ▪ 1870-1965

American cosmetics executive born in Poland. In Australia she marketed face cream brewed by a Hungarian doctor, and its success was the beginning of the $100 million business empire of which she was founder and president. She wrote her memoirs in her 90s.

REGARDING OLD AGE:

"It seems the older I get, the more I have to do."

AT AGE 94:

"I have always felt that a woman has the right to treat the subject of her age with ambiguity until, perhaps, she passes into the realm of over 90. Then it is better she be candid with herself and with the world."

ARTHUR RUBINSTEIN ▪ 1887–1982

Polish-born American concert pianist. A child prodigy who performed his first concert at age 5, he had a career that spanned nearly 90 years, the longest to date in the history of music.

REGARDING OLD AGE:

> **"When I was young, I used to have successes with women because I was young. Now I have successes with women because I am old. Middle age was the hard part."**

AT AGE 91:

> **"I did affirm to my readers in *My Young Years* that I was the happiest man I had ever met, and I can profoundly reaffirm it at the age of 91."**

AT AGE 93, ON HIS FINAL CONCERT IN LONDON'S
WIGMORE HALL, WHERE HE HAD GIVEN HIS FIRST RECITAL:

"The first movement represented the struggles of my youth, the following andante the beginning of a more serious aspect of my talent, a scherzo represented well the unexpected success, and the finale turned out to be a wonderfully moving end."

Bertrand Russell ▪ 1872-1970

English philosopher and mathematician. At 79 he received the Nobel Prize in Literature for his *History of Western Philosophy*.

At age 66:

> **"To acquire immunity to eloquence is of the utmost importance to the citizens of a democracy."**

At age 78:

> **"Fear is the main source of superstition, and one of the main sources of cruelty. To conquer fear is the beginning of wisdom."**

At age 80:

> **"The boa constrictor, when he has had an adequate meal, goes to sleep and does not wake until he needs another meal. Human beings, for the most part, are not like this."**

At age 87:

> "I agree that being thrown to the wolves
> is tedious, but after 87 years of it my re-
> actions are no longer so vehement."

At age 94:

> "Three passions have governed my life:
> the longing for love, the search for
> knowledge, and the unbearable pity for
> the suffering of mankind."

At age 97, to his wife, a month before he died:

> "I do so hate to leave this world."

Camille Saint-Saëns • 1835-1921

French composer. A child prodigy, he made his debut as a pianist at 10 and was organist at the Church of the Madeleine for 20 years. He is best known for his biblical opera, *Samson et Dalila*.

At age 85:

> **"The harvest is gathered in. At the age of 85 one has the right, perhaps the duty, of falling silent."**

CARL SANDBURG ▪ 1878-1967

American poet, biographer, and folklorist. His vigorous free verse celebrated America and its common people.

AT AGE 70:

"A baby is God's opinion that life should go on."

AT AGE 81:

"Slang is a language that rolls up its sleeves, spits on its hands, and goes to work."

George Santayana ▪ 1863-1952

U.S. philosophical writer and essayist, born in Spain and raised in the U.S. He taught at Harvard.

REGARDING OLD AGE:

> **"Old persons have an intrinsic value of which youth is incapable; precisely the balance and wisdom that come from long perspectives and broad foundations."**

REGARDING HIS OLD AGE:

> **"My old age judges more charitably and thinks better of mankind than my youth ever did."**

AT AGE 62:

> **"The young man who has not wept is a savage, and the old man who will not laugh is a fool."**

AT AGE 72:

> **"The primary use of conversation is to satisfy the impulse to talk."**

MAY SARTON ▪ 1912-

American poet, novelist, and essayist. Much of her work concerns aging.

AT AGE 61:

> **"How unnatural the imposed view . . . that passionate love belongs only to the young."**

AT AGE 70:

> **"Old age is not an illness, it is a timeless ascent. As power diminishes, we grow toward the light."**

ELSA SCHIAPARELLI ▪ 1890-1973

Italian-French fashion designer. Noted for her flamboyant, daring innovations, she used brilliant colors such as "shocking pink" and introduced padded shoulders, synthetic fabric, and zippers.

AT AGE 64:

"A good cook is like a sorceress who dispenses happiness."

"Fashion is born by small facts, trends, or even politics, never by trying to make little pleats, by trinkets, by clothes easy to copy, or by the shortening or lengthening of a skirt."

ALBERT SCHWEITZER ▪ 1875-1965

Alsatian philosopher, musician, and physician. He won the 1952 Nobel Peace Prize after giving up the life of a scholar and organist to become a medical missionary in French equatorial Africa.

AT AGE 74:

"Truth has no special time of its own. Its hour is now—always."

AT AGE 80:

"An optimist is a person who sees a green light everywhere, while the pessimist sees only the red stoplight. . . . The truly wise person is color-blind."

AT AGE 81:

"Reverence for life affords me my fundamental principle of morality."

AT AGE 83:

"By practicing reverence for life we become good, deep, and alive."

FLORIDA SCOTT-MAXWELL •
1883-1978

American playwright and novelist who was an active participant in the early women's liberation movement. She started her journal, *The Measure of My Days*, at age 82, and it was published three years later.

REGARDING OLD AGE:

"We who are old know that age is more than a disability. It is an intense and varied experience, almost beyond capacity at times, but something to be carried high."

"I want to tell people approaching and perhaps fearing age that it is a time of discovery."

At age 82:

> "Age puzzles me. I thought it was a quiet time. My 70s were interesting and fairly serene, but my 80s are passionate. I grow more intense as I age."

At age 85:

> "The crucial task of old age is balance: keeping just well enough, just brave enough, just gay and interested and starkly honest enough to remain a sentient human being."

George Bernard Shaw ▪ 1856-1950

Irish dramatist, critic, social reformer, and novelist. At age 69 he was awarded a Nobel Prize.

REGARDING OLD AGE:

> **"All that the young can do for the old is to shock them and keep them up to date."**

REGARDING HIS OLD AGE:

> **"I want to be thoroughly used up when I die, for the harder I work, the more I live."**

AT AGE 67:

> **"It is difficult, if not impossible, for most people to think otherwise than in the fashion of their own period."**

AT AGE 88:

> **"A government which robs Peter to pay Paul can always depend on the support of Paul."**

> **"Nonsense, I look exactly like a man of 90 should look. Everyone else looks older because of the dissolute lives they lead."**

BISHOP FULTON SHEEN ▪ 1895-1979

American Roman Catholic bishop. An outstanding orator, he was well known for his radio and television broadcasts as well as for his attacks on Communism and Freudian psychology.

AT AGE 60:

> **"An atheist is a man who has no invisible means of support."**

AT AGE 77:

> **"Jealousy is the tribute mediocrity pays to genius."**

Jean Sibelius ▪ 1865-1957

Finnish master composer and principal creator of Finnish national music.

AT AGE 91:

"Every day in my old age is more important than I can say. It will never return. When one takes one's leave of life one notices how much one has left undone."

Georges Simenon ▪ 1903-1989

Belgian-French novelist who produced hundreds of short stories and books. Writing under at least 17 pseudonyms, he became one of the most widely published authors of the century.

AT AGE 78:

"I adore life but I don't fear death. I just prefer to die as late as possible."

Isaac Bashevis Singer ▪ 1904-1991

Polish-American novelist and short-story writer. He wrote children's stories and serialized novels, all in Yiddish. In 1978 he was awarded the Nobel Prize in Literature.

REGARDING OLD AGE:

> **"Literature has neglected the old and their emotions. The novelist never told us that in life, as in other matters, the young are just beginners and that the art of loving matures with age and experience."**

AT AGE 74:

> **"Literature is the memory of humanity."**

> **"It seems that analysis of character is the highest form of human entertainment. And literature does it, unlike gossip, without mentioning real names."**

B. F. SKINNER ▪ 1904-1990

U.S. behavioral psychologist. He was a pioneer in the study of human behavior in terms of measurable responses to stimuli.

AT AGE 60:

"Education is what survives when what has been learnt has been forgotten."

AT AGE 64:

"The real problem is not whether machines think, but whether men do."

Anglo-American author, essayist, and critic. Born in the U.S., he lived in England and studied at Oxford. He wrote his autobiography at age 74.

AT AGE 66:

"There are two things to aim at in life: first, to get what you want and, after that, to enjoy it. Only the wisest of mankind achieve the second."

"The denunciation of the young is a necessary part of the hygiene of older people and greatly assists in the circulation of the blood."

"We need two kinds of acquaintances: one to complain to; to the second, we boast."

"Happiness is a wine of rarest vintage, and seems insipid to a vulgar taste."

"Charming people live up to the very edge of their charm, and behave as outrageously as the world lets them."

"There are people who, like houses, are beautiful in dilapidation."

"The test of a vocation is the love of the drudgery it involves."

At age 68:

"The mere process of growing old together will make the slightest acquaintance seem a bosom friend."

"Don't let young people tell you their aspirations; when they drop them they will drop you."

"Growing old is no gradual decline, but a series of tumbles from one ledge to another. Yet when we pick ourselves up we find no bones are broken; while not unpleasing is the new terrace which stretches out unexplored before us."

MARGARET CHASE SMITH ▪ 1897-

U.S. politician and columnist. The first congresswoman and the first female senator from Maine, she served longer in the Senate than any other woman (1949-73).

AT AGE 67, ANNOUNCING HER PRESIDENTIAL CANDIDACY:

"When people keep telling you that you can't do a thing, you kind of like to try it."

Dr. Benjamin Spock ▪ 1903-

U.S. pediatrician. His *Common Sense Book of Baby and Child Care* (1946) has sold more than 25 million copies.

AT AGE 65:

"Successful marriage is an art that can only be learned with difficulty. But it gives pride and satisfaction, like any other expertness that is hard won."

"I would say that the surest measure of a man's or a woman's maturity is the harmony, style, joy, and dignity he creates in his marriage, and the pleasure and inspiration he provides for his spouse."

Elizabeth Cady Stanton ■ 1815-1902

American social reformer. A leader of the women's-suffrage movement, she helped organize the first convention dealing with women's rights (1848).

AT AGE 66:

> **"The prolonged slavery of women is the darkest page in human history."**

> **"Womanhood is the great fact in her life; wifehood and motherhood are but incidental relations."**

Freya Stark ▪ 1893-1993

British travel writer.

AT AGE 70:

"Good days are to be gathered like sunshine in grapes, to be trodden and bottled into wine and kept for age to sip at ease beside the fire. If the traveler has vintaged well, he need trouble to wander no longer; the ruby moments glow in his glass at will."

"On the whole, age comes more gently to those who have some doorway into an abstract world—art, or philosophy, or learning—regions where the years are scarcely noticed and the young and old can meet in a pale truthful light."

WALLACE STEGNER ▪ 1909-1993

American author, educator, historian, and biographer.

AT AGE 67:

> **"The lessons of life amount not to wisdom but to scar tissue and callus."**

> **"It is something—it can be everything—to have found a fellow bird with whom you can sit among the rafters while the drinking and boasting and reciting and fighting go on below."**

EDWARD STEICHEN ▪ 1879-1973

U.S. celebrity photographer who, with Stieglitz, founded the Photo-Secession Gallery in 1905.

AT AGE 82:

"Photography is a major force in explaining man to man."

"Photography records the gamut of feelings written on the human face, the beauty of the earth and skies that man has inherited, and the wealth and confusion man has created."

JIMMY STEWART ▪ 1908-

A leading man in American movies. He is famous for his slow drawl and shy, homespun charm.

REGARDING OLD AGE:

"After age 70 it's patch, patch, patch."

AT AGE 78:

"It's well done if you can do a part and not have the acting show."

I. F. STONE ▪ 1907-1989

U.S. journalist and publisher. He organized the all-American Youth Orchestra, a forum for young performers, and formed the American Symphony Orchestra.

AT AGE 77:

"The biggest difference between ancient Rome and the U.S.A. is that in Rome the common man was treated like a dog. In America he sets the tone."

AT AGE 81:

"When you are younger you get blamed for crimes you never committed and when you're older you begin to get credit for virtues you never possessed. It evens itself out."

Harriet Beecher Stowe ▪ 1811-1896

American author whose antislavery novel, *Uncle Tom's Cabin* (1852), enlisted sympathy for the cause of abolition.

REGARDING OLD AGE:

"So much has been said and sung of beautiful young girls, why doesn't somebody wake up to the beauty of old women?"

Igor Stravinsky ▪ 1882-1971

Russian-American composer. He is best known for his ballets including *The Firebird* and *Petrouchka*. His use of irregular primitive rhythms and harsh dissonances profoundly influenced two generations of musicians.

AT AGE 75:

"To listen is an effort, and just to hear is no merit. A duck hears also."

ALBERT SZENT-GYÖRGYI ▪ 1893-1986

Hungarian-American biochemist. He was the first to isolate vitamin C, although he failed to identify it as such. He was awarded the 1937 Nobel Prize in Physiology or Medicine.

AT AGE 69:

> **"Discovery consists of seeing what everybody has seen and thinking what nobody has thought."**

Jessica Tandy · 1909-1994

English actress known for her long stage career, mostly with her husband, Hume Cronyn. She received a Best Actress Award for *A Streetcar Named Desire* (1948) and an Oscar for her role in *Driving Miss Daisy* (1989).

At age 83:

"I think we are able to keep active longer provided we approach our lives with creativity. I think the mere fact that we keep doing is self-creating."

"You can always learn new ways of doing things. If you are set in your ways and simply repeat things over and over, whatever you do will become stale. Each new project must be attacked as though it were a first effort."

"Each of us must do whatever we have a passion to do."

Edward Teller · 1908-

American physicist born in Hungary. He is called "Father of the H-Bomb" for devising a secret element that made the hydrogen bomb practical.

AT AGE 72:

> **"Life improves slowly and goes wrong fast, and only catastrophe is clearly visible."**

> **"No endeavor that is worthwhile is simple in prospect; if it is right, it will be simple in retrospect."**

> **"History, most often, is recorded with a great amount of undeniable and systematic distortion."**

AT AGE 77:

> **"When you fight for a desperate cause and have good reasons to fight, you usually win."**

ALFRED, LORD TENNYSON •
1809-1892

The most famous English poet of the Victorian era. He was Poet Laureate of England for 42 years.

ON OLD AGE:

". . . you and I are old . . .
Though much is taken, much abides;
and though
We are not now that strength which in
the old days
Moved earth and heaven, that which we
are, we are
One equal temper of heroic hearts."

MOTHER TERESA ▪ 1910-

Albanian-born Roman Catholic missionary. Born Agnes Gonxha Bojaxhiu, she is widely respected for international humanitarian efforts for the poor and disenfranchised. She was awarded the Nobel Peace Prize in 1979.

AT AGE 65:

"Loneliness and the feeling of being unwanted is the most terrible poverty."

"We ourselves feel that what we are doing is just a drop in the ocean. But if that drop was not in the ocean, I think the ocean would be less because of that missing drop. I do not agree with the big way of doing things."

"Even the rich are hungry for love, for being cared for, for being wanted, for having someone to call their own."

At age 71:

> **"I have found the paradox that if I love until it hurts, then there is no hurt, but only more love."**

Dr. Lewis Thomas ▪ 1913-1993

U.S. physician and educator. He was president of the Memorial Sloan-Kettering Institute for Cancer Research.

AT AGE 61:

> **"The uniformity of earth's life is accountable by the high probability that we derived from some single cell fertilized in a bolt of lightning as the earth cooled."**

AT AGE 63:

> **"The great secret of doctors . . . is that most things get better by themselves; most things, in fact, are better in the morning."**

AT AGE 66:

> **"We are, perhaps uniquely among the earth's creatures, the worrying animal."**

> **"We are built to make mistakes, coded for error."**

LOWELL THOMAS ▪ 1892-1981

World traveler, reporter, editor, and radio newscaster for more than 50 years. He is said to have been the first to broadcast from a ship, an airplane, a submarine, and a coal mine.

AT AGE 86:

"After the age of 80, everything reminds you of something else."

NORMAN THOMAS ▪ 1884-1968

U.S. Socialist leader, reformer, editor, and minister. He helped found the American Civil Liberties Union and was a frequent presidential candidate.

AT AGE 73, TO ANTI-NUCLEAR BOMB DEMONSTRATORS:

"I'd rather see America save her soul than her face."

Dame Sybil Thorndike ▪ 1882–1976

English actress. At age 87, she performed at the opening of the London theater named for her.

AT AGE 79, AFTER THE FLOP OF *VANITY FAIR*, A MUSICAL IN WHICH SHE HAD DANCED AND SUNG:

> **"One should never be sorry one has attempted something new—never, never, never."**

Josef Broz Tito ▪ 1892–1980

Yugoslav leader. After being imprisoned as a political agitator, he was repeatedly elected Communist president from 1953, at age 61, until his death at age 87.

AT AGE 61:

> **"Men make history and play a considerable part in it only if they understand the people's needs and wishes, and insofar as they become part of the people themselves."**

J. R. R. Tolkien ▪ 1892-1973

English author and scholar born in South Africa. His adult fairy tales gained great popularity during the 1960s.

At age 62:

> **"All that is gold does not glitter; not all those that wander are lost."**

LEO TOLSTOY ▪ 1828-1910

Russian novelist. His works have been translated into nearly every Western language.

AT AGE 64:

> **"The more is given the less people will work for themselves, and the less they work the more their poverty will increase."**

AT AGE 70:

> **"Art is a human activity having for its purpose the transmission to others of the highest and best feelings to which men have risen."**

> **"Art transmits truths from the region of perception to the region of emotion."**

> **"To say that a work of art is good, but incomprehensible to the majority of men, is the same as saying of some kind of food that it is very good but that most people can't eat it."**

AT AGE 78:

> **"Don't complain about old age. How much good it has brought me that was unexpected and beautiful. I concluded from that that the end of old age and life will be just as unexpectedly beautiful."**

Arnold J. Toynbee ▪ 1889-1975

English historian, and author of the 12-volume *A Study of History*.

AT AGE 65:

> **"America is a large friendly dog in a small room. Every time it wags its tail it knocks over a chair."**

AT AGE 66:

> **"History not used is nothing, for all intellectual life is action and if you don't use the stuff—well, it might as well be dead."**

AT AGE 69:

> **"Civilization is a movement and not a condition, a voyage and not a harbor."**

AT AGE 85:

> **"The right moment for starting on your next job is not tomorrow or next week; it is *instanter*, or in the American idiom, '*right now*.'"**

BEN TRAVERS ▪ 1886-1980

English dramatist.

AT AGE 93:

"But I'll tell you the really great thing about living to be 93: One does not have any rivals, because they're all dead, so one can afford to be generous."

BESS TRUMAN ▪ 1885-1982

The wife of Harry S. Truman, thirty-third president of the U.S.

AT AGE 60:

"I deplore any action which denies artistic talent an opportunity to express itself because of prejudice against race origin."

Harry S. Truman · 1884-1972

Thirty-third U.S. president, who took office on the death of Franklin D. Roosevelt.

AT AGE 71:

"I have found the best way to give advice to your children is to find out what they want and then advise them to do it."

AT AGE 74:

"I never did give anybody hell. I just told the truth and they thought it was hell."

"A politician is a man who understands government, and it takes a politician to run the government."

AT AGE 80, ON HOW TO REACH THAT AGE:

"Pick the right grandparents, don't eat or drink too much, be circumspect in all things, and take a two-mile walk every morning before breakfast."

Louis Untermeyer ■ 1885-1977

U.S. poet, editor, and writer. He is best known for his anthologies.

AT AGE 80:

> "It is not easy to hear a poet's voice in such a world. Nevertheless, the poet somehow manages to make himself heard, chiefly because people want to hear him."

> "I take inordinate pleasure in the ready response of the five lively senses and wish that the sixth sense, the sense of knowing, was equally quick."

GIUSEPPE VERDI ▪ 1813-1901

Foremost Italian composer of opera. *Otello* and *Falstaff*, finished when he was 73 and 80, respectively, are considered the masterpieces of his old age.

AT AGE 82, REGARDING CRITICS:

"To be esteemed and loved you need to grow old."

AT AGE 88, SHORTLY BEFORE HIS DEATH:

"When writing music . . . write as you feel, without fear, and be sincere."

ELIZABETH GRAY VINING ▪ 1902-

American author and tutor to Crown Prince Akihito of Japan.

AT AGE 70:

> **"I am old in years and in the sight of others, but I do not feel old within myself. I have hopes and purposes, things to do before I die. A surging of life within me cries 'Not yet! Not yet!'"**

François Marie de Voltaire ▪ 1694-1778

French philosopher who called for tolerance, humanity, and justice. His works are contained in more than 90 volumes of poetry, plays, prose, and historical essays. At 64 he published his most popular work, the play *Candide.*

AT AGE 65:

"Work keeps us from three great evils: boredom, vice, and poverty."

AT AGE 70:

"Common sense is not so common."

"One merit of poetry few persons will deny: It says more and in fewer words than prose."

"Men who are occupied in the restoration of health of other men, by the joint exertion of skill and humanity, are above all the great of the earth. They can even partake of divinity, since to preserve and renew is almost as noble as to create."

"In general, the art of government consists in taking as much money as possible from one party of the citizens to give to the other."

AT AGE 82:

"I am very fond of the truth, but not at all of martyrdom."

AT AGE 84:

"I die adoring God, loving my friends, not hating my enemies, and detesting superstition."

Izaak Walton ▪ 1593-1683

English writer best known as the author of *The Compleat Angler,* a discourse on the pleasures of fishing.

AT AGE 60:

"I have laid aside business, and gone a-fishing."

"Good company and good discourse are the very sinews of virtue."

Sylvia Townsend Warner ▪ 1893-1978

English novelist, short-story writer, and poet.

REGARDING AGING:

> "Time sweeps one on, sweeps one into the enthusiasms of one's adolescence and out of them into fresh enthusiasms."

AT AGE 73:

> "You are only young once. At the time it seems endless and is gone in a flash; and then for a very long time you are old."

Earl Warren ▪ 1891-1974

Governor of California and chief justice of the Supreme Court. He presided over a period of great change in civil rights, and wrote the Supreme Court decision regarding school desegregation.

AT AGE 63:

> **"We conclude that in the field of public education the doctrine of 'separate but equal' has no place. Separate educational facilities are inherently unequal."**

NOAH WEBSTER ▪ 1758-1843

American teacher and journalist who compiled the earliest American dictionaries of the English language.

AT AGE 77:

> **"I began life, as other young men do, full of confidence in my own opinions, many of which I afterwards found to be visionary and deceptive. . . . To err is the lot of humanity."**

Arthur Wellesley Wellington, the first Duke of Wellington. He was an army field marshal, statesman, and prime minister.

AT AGE 62:

"The only thing I am afraid of is fear."

AT AGE 65:

"My rule always was to do the business of the day in the day."

Eudora Welty ▪ 1909-

American short-story writer and novelist who often writes about the inhabitants of rural Mississippi. She was awarded a Pulitzer Prize in Fiction in 1972.

At age 75:

> "Writing fiction has developed in me an abiding respect for the unknown in a human lifetime and a sense of where to look for the threads. The strands are all there: To the memory nothing is ever really lost."

> "I am a writer who came of a sheltered life. A sheltered life can be a daring life as well. For all serious daring starts from within."

John Wesley ▪ 1703-1791

British evangelist and founder of Methodism. He and his group were derisively called "methodists" for their methodical devotion to study and religious duties.

At age 75:

> **"Once in seven years I burn all my sermons; for it is a shame if I cannot write better sermons now than I did seven years ago."**

Jessamyn West · 1902-1984

American writer.

AT AGE 60:

"We want the facts to fit the preconceptions. When they don't, it is easier to ignore the facts than to change the preconceptions."

AT AGE 71:

"Fiction reveals truths that reality obscures."

AT AGE 77:

"Memory is a magnet. It will pull to it and hold only material nature has designed it to attract."

MAE WEST ▪ 1892-1980

Bawdy American entertainer who began her career in burlesque. She wrote and starred in her own Broadway plays and was still acting in her 80s.

REGARDING AGING:

"You're never too old to become younger."

AT AGE 67:

"I have never posed as the definitive expert on the sexes, but I have done my own field work."

AT AGE 73:

"Sex is an emotion in motion."

AT AGE 78:

"Personally, the only four-letter word I would use is love."

"My life has been a splendid prelude for what I hope to do."

AT AGE 83:

"There are no good girls gone wrong, just bad girls found out."

"When it comes to finances, remember that there are no withholding taxes on the wages of sin."

DAME REBECCA WEST ▪ 1892-1983

English author, literary critic, and prize-winning journalist for her reports on the Nuremberg war-crimes trials.

AT AGE 65:

> **"Any authentic work of art must start an argument between the artist and his audience."**

AT AGE 82:

> **"You couldn't live 82 years in the world without being disillusioned."**

AT AGE 83:

> **"Everyone realizes that one can believe little of what people say about each other. But it is not so widely realized that even less can one trust what people say about themselves."**

John Hall Wheelock · 1886-1978

American poet and administrator at the Library of Congress.

AT AGE 90:

"You don't feel you are any older, but suddenly you realize you are. But instead of life getting dimmer and duller, it gets so poignant it's unbearable. Like looking at the sun, you can't stand it because it's unbearable."

E. B. WHITE ▪ 1899-1985

American humorist, essayist, and novelist who was a witty, satiric observer of the contemporary scene. His children's books have become classics.

AT AGE 62:

"There is a period near the beginning of every man's life when he has little to cling to except his unmanageable dream, little to support him except good health, and nowhere to go but all over the place."

AT AGE 78:

"The essayist can put on any sort of shirt, be any sort of person, according to his mood or his subject matter—philosopher, scold, jester, raconteur, confidant, pundit, devil's advocate, enthusiast."

ALFRED NORTH WHITEHEAD •
1861-1947

English mathematician and philosopher. He wrote, with Bertrand Russell, the three-volume *Principia Mathematica*, a landmark in the study of logic.

AT AGE 77:

"The vitality of thought is in adventure. Ideas won't keep. Something must be done about them."

AT AGE 80:

"What is morality in any given time or place? It is what the majority then and there happen to like, and immorality is what they dislike."

AT AGE 82:

"Art is the imposing of a pattern on experience, and our aesthetic enjoyment is recognition of the pattern."

Billy Wilder ▪ 1906-1992

Austrian-born American film director, producer, and writer. In 1945 *The Lost Weekend* won him Academy Awards for best direction, best picture, and best screenplay.

AT AGE 76, ON REFUSING RETIREMENT:

"As far as I'm concerned, this ball game is not over. . . . There are still a few hits left in me."

AT AGE 86:

"An audience is never wrong. An individual member of it may be an imbecile, but a thousand imbeciles together in the dark—that is critical genius."

WALTER WINCHELL ▪ 1879-1972

American journalist, radio broadcaster, and gossip columnist.

AT AGE 71:

> **"When you reach 70 you shrug at everything; so what?"**

P. G. WODEHOUSE ▪ 1881-1975

English novelist, short-story writer, playwright, and screenwriter best known for his farces about English gentry in the Edwardian era.

AT AGE 92:

> **"The trouble about reaching the age of 92 is that regrets for a misspent life are bound to creep in."**

Frank Lloyd Wright • 1867-1959

American architect whose influence can be seen in Japan, the Netherlands, France, and Germany. His Guggenheim Museum in New York was completed when he was 91.

REGARDING OLD AGE:

"The longer I live the more beautiful life becomes."

AT AGE 65:

"No house should ever be *on* a hill or *on* anything. It should be *of* the hill. Belonging to it."

AT AGE 86:

"The physician can bury his mistakes, but the architect can only advise his client to plant vines."

> **"No science can be humanely fruitful until art, religion, philosophy, ethics, and science are comprehended as one great entity, a universal unity seen as the Beautiful."**

EDWARD YOUNG ■ 1683-1765

English poet and dramatist famous for his long poems. He also wrote satires.

AT AGE 60:

> **"All men think all men mortal, but themselves."**

> **"Procrastination is the thief of time."**

> **"Like our shadows,**
> **Our wishes lengthen**
> **as the sun declines."**

ADOLPH ZUKOR ▪ 1873-1976

U.S. film executive born in Hungary. He founded the company which eventually, through mergers, became Paramount Pictures and was promoter of the first full-length feature film, *Queen Elizabeth*, starring Sarah Bernhardt.

AT AGE 98:

> **"I sleep well because I don't let my mind get stale."**

References

Adams, Abby, comp. *An Uncommon Scold*. New York: Simon and Schuster, 1989.

Amory, Cleveland, ed. *The International Celebrity Register*. New York: Simon and Schuster, 1959.

Andrews, Robert, comp. *The Concise Columbia Dictionary of Quotations*. New York: Columbia University Press, 1989.

Auden, W. H., and Louis Kronenberger, eds. *The Viking Book of Aphorisms*. New York: Penguin Books, 1962.

Augarde, Tony, ed. *The Oxford Dictionary of Modern Quotations*. New York: Oxford University Press, 1991.

Berman, Phillip L., and Connie Goldman, eds. *The Ageless Spirit*. New York: Ballantine, 1992.

Bohle, Bruce, comp. *The Home Book of American Quotations*. New York: Donald Mead, 1967.

Boorstin, Daniel J. *The Creators*. New York: Random House, 1992.

Brockway, Wallace, and Bart Keith. *A Second Treasury of the World's Great Letters*. New York: Winer, 1941.

Bronaugh, Robert Brett, comp. *The Celebrity Birthday Book*. New York: J. David, 1981.

Byrne, Robert. *The Fourth and by Far the Most Recent 637 Best Things Anybody Ever Said*. New York: Fawcett, 1990.

Chase's Annual Events 1992. Chicago: Contemporary Books, 1992.

Ciardi, John. *A Browser's Dictionary*. Harper and Row, 1980.

Comfort, Alex. *A Good Age*. New York: Crown Publishers, 1977.

Conlin, Joseph R. *The Morrow Book of Quotations in American History*. New York: Morrow, 1984.

Crofton, Ian, and Donald Fraser. *A Dictionary of Musical Quotations*. New York: Schirmer Books, 1985.

Donadio, Stephen, et al., eds. *The New York Library Book*

of *20th-Century American Quotations*. New York: Prentice Hall, 1992.

Earl Blackwell's Entertainment Celebrity Register. New York: Visible Ink Press, 1990.

Evans, Bergen, comp. *Dictionary of Quotations*. New York: Outlet Book Co., 1968.

Fadiman, Clifton, ed. *The Little, Brown Book of Anecdotes*. New York: Little, Brown, 1985.

Flexner, Stuart B. *I Hear America Talking*. New York: Van Nostrand Reinhold, 1976.

Fowler, Margaret, and Priscilla McCutcheon, eds. *Songs of Experience: An Anthology of Literature on Growing Old*. New York: Ballantine, 1991.

Gardner, John W., and Francesca Reese. *Quotations of Wit and Wisdom*. New York: Norton, 1980.

Green, Jonathon, comp. *Morrow's International Dictionary of Contemporary Quotations*. New York: Morrow, 1982.

Gross, John, comp. *The Oxford Book of Aphorisms*. New York: Oxford University Press, 1983.

Harris, William B., and Judith S. Levy, eds. *The New Co-*

lumbia Encyclopedia. New York: Columbia University Press, 1975.

Hirsch, E. D., Jr. *A Dictionary of Cultural Literacy.* Boston: Houghton Mifflin, 1988.

Hurd, Charles. *A Treasury of Great American Quotations.* New York: Hawthorne Books, 1964.

Kaditsky, Jill, ed. *Current Biography Cumulated Index 1940–1990.* New York: Wilson, 1991.

Kanin, Garson. *It Takes a Long Time to Become Young.* Boston: G. K. Hall, 1978.

Kaplan, Justin, ed. *Bartlett's Familiar Quotations.* Boston: Little, Brown and Co., 1992.

Kemble, Frances Anne (Fanny). *A Journal of a Residence on a Georgian Plantation in 1838–1839.* New York: Alfred A. Knopf, 1961.

King, Anita, comp. and ed. *Quotations in Black.* Westport, Connecticut: Greenwood Press, 1981.

Lane, Hana Umlauf, ed. *The World Almanac Book of Who.* New York: World Almanac Publications, 1980.

Larsen, Stephen, and Robin Larsen. *A Fire in the Mind: The Life of Joseph Campbell.* New York: Doubleday, 1991.

Levinson, Leonard Louis. *Bartlett's Unfamiliar Quotations*. Chicago: Cowles Book Co., 1977.

The Macmillan Dictionary of Quotations. New York: Macmillan, 1989.

Maggio, Rosalie, comp. *The Beacon Book of Quotations by Women*. Boston: Beacon Press, 1992.

McFarlan, Donald, ed. *The Guinness Book of Records*. New York: Bantam, 1991.

Morris, Desmond. *The Book of Ages*. New York: Ballantine, 1983.

The New York Library Book of Chronologies. New York: Prentice Hall, 1990.

Partington, Angela, ed. *The Oxford Dictionary of Quotations*. New York: Oxford University Press, 1992.

Peter, Lawrence J. *Peter's Quotations: Ideas for Our Time*. New York: Bantam, 1983.

Platt, Suzy, ed. *Respectfully Quoted*. Washington: Library of Congress, 1989.

Partnow, Elaine, comp. and ed. *The New Quotable Women 1800–1975*. New York: Facts on File, 1992.

Prochnow, Herbert V., and Herbert V. Prochnow, Jr. *The*

Public Speaker's Treasure Chest. 4th ed. New York: Harper and Row, 1986.

Rawson, Hugh, and Margaret Miner, eds. *The New International Dictionary of Quotations*. New York: NAL-Dutton, 1986.

Reflections: A Woman's Own Journal with Illustrations and Quotes. New York: Running Press, 1987.

Sampson, Anthony, and Sally Sampson, comps. *The Oxford Book of Ages*. Oxford and New York: Oxford University Press, 1985.

Schlueter, Paul, and June Schlueter, eds. *An Encyclopedia of British Women Writers*. New York and London: Garland Press, 1988.

Seldes, George, comp. *The Great Quotations*. New York: Carol Publishing, 1983.

Shipps, Anthony W. *The Quote Slueth: A Manual for the Tracer of Lost Quotations*. Chicago: University of Illinois Press, 1990.

Simpson, James B., comp. *Simpson's Contemporary Quotations*. Boston: Houghton Mifflin, 1988.

Stetler, Susan, ed. *Almanac of Famous People*. Detroit: Gale Research, 1989.

Thomas, Henry, and Dan Lee Thomas. *Living Biographies of Great Philosophers*. New York: Garden City Publishing Co., 1959.

Untermeyer, Louis. *The Britannica Library of Great American Writing*. New York: Britannica Press, 1960.

Uris, Dorothy. *Say It Again: Dorothy Uris' Personal Collection of Quotes, Comments & Anecdotes*. New York: E. P. Dutton, 1979.

Ventura, Piero. *Great Composers*. New York: Putnam, 1988.

Vernoff, Edward, and Rema Shore. *The International Dictionary of 20th Century Biography*. New York: NAL-Dutton, 1987.

Winokur, Jon, comp. and ed. *The Portable Curmudgeon*. New York: NAL Penguin, 1987.

Winokur, Jon, comp. *True Confessions*. New York: Penguin Books, 1992.

About the Authors

GRETCHEN B. DIANDA has been an active environmentalist for many years and lives with her family in San Francisco. Formerly a radio and TV journalist, she often works with her father, Walter M. Bortz, M.D., one of the nation's leading geriatricians.

BETTY J. HOFMAYER graduated from Stanford University with a degree in history. Since then she has been a researcher for Time, Inc., Hiller Aircraft, several writers, and most recently, educational software for children. She and her husband live in Palo Alto. They have two children and four grandchildren.